VINCE DOOLEY'S
Garden

Happy Gardening

Vince Dooley

VINCE DOOLEY'S
Garden

THE HORTICULTURAL JOURNEY OF A FOOTBALL COACH

with paintings by STEVE PENLEY

I would like to express my heartfelt thanks to all who have helped me in this journey
and in guiding me through the process of creating this book,
especially Dr. Michael Dirr and Dr. Allan Armitage.

My appreciation also goes to Julie Taylor who typed (and re-typed) the manuscript.

Published by
Looking Glass Books, Inc.
Decatur, Georgia

Distributed by John F. Blair, Publisher

Text copyright © 2010 Vince Dooley
Paintings and illustrations © 2010 Steve Penley

Photography by Dr. Michael Dirr, except

Teresa Penley Sheppard: pages 22, 23, 93, 94, 95, 121, 126,
135, 136, 137, 138, 139, 149, 142, 143, 144, 152

Garden plan views by Gregg Coyle: pages 114, 122, 145

ISBN 978-1-929619-37-5

Manufactured in Canada

Book and jacket design by Burtch Hunter Design

With love and appreciation to my wife, Barbara, in celebration of our 50th wedding anniversary.

FOREWORD

MICHAEL A. DIRR, Ph.D.

A football coach and athletic director at a major university falls head-over-spade in love with gardening. Too far-fetched to have any basis in reality? Allow me to guide the reader along the never-ending garden path forged by Coach Vincent J. Dooley, University of Georgia.

First, several caveats concerning Coach's remarkable attributes: great love for family; noble affection for the University of Georgia; willingness to assist with any project that benefits the greater good; renaissance inquisitiveness about art, literature, and history; and indefatigable energy. Integrity and hope undergird this rich, full, and accomplished life.

Enter gardening and horticulture into this domain circa 1995–96 when he audited my woody plant courses. Lectures, laboratories, field trips . . . he seldom missed. The seeds were planted in the classroom, but the development, growth, and fruition took hold at 755 Milledge Circle, Coach's home and perpetually evolving garden.

There were numerous throwaway plants from my plant breeding and evaluation program. Coach was always receptive to the extras, and his garden is now rich with unnamed seedlings that, on occasion, matured to magnificent plants. Sheepishly, I now ask for cuttings of the superior selections. Coach's favorite retort . . . "Help yourself." Great gardeners, if they have two of anything, always share.

The garden grows and space becomes limited. Coach, during his travels, visits nurseries and garden centers. Every new plant deserves testing in the Dooley garden. His collection of woody plants now supersedes any in the Athens area. Plants are labeled and mapped. As additional land becomes available, plants appear to have legs. I query Coach about a viburnum. "Needed space, so I moved it," was his answer.

Barbara believes the gardening activities are now spinning out of control. New paths, water features, sunroom, gazebo, and containers keep appearing. The containers, perhaps in the hundreds, are quickly filled with a plethora of rare woody plants. Japanese maples, well over one hundred, dot the garden. *Hydrangea macrophylla* 'Dooley', a cold-hardy selection from his garden, is now ensconced in major nurseries and gardens.

The legend grows and Coach is now on the garden lecture circuit. Every horticulturist who visits Athens asks to see Coach's garden. Coach describes this incredible transformation as an unending journey. The process (never-ending), the people (always intriguing), the plant palette (ever-expanding), and the anticipation (hope springs eternal) are brought to exuberant life in this book through the experiences of a great football coach—now a great gardener.

VINCE DOOLEY'S
Garden

CHAPTER ONE

THE JOURNEY BEGINS

THE JOY OF LEARNING

I embarked on this horticulture journey some twelve years ago while taking advantage of the special learning rewards that come with living around a university. I have had the good fortune of university life for some sixty years, combining my time both at Auburn University and the University of Georgia. This lengthy academic environment has given me a real appreciation of the joy of learning, which was not always the case growing up.

I was fortunate to have been raised by parents with solid Christian values; however, neither my mom nor dad had formal education beyond the grammar school level. I attended a Catholic boys school taught by the Brothers of the Sacred Heart, who were strict disciplinarians, demanding that lessons be learned the old-fashioned way. I did not particularly like school and did only what was necessary to graduate so I would not have to go to school again.

But thanks to my love of sports and the influence of a good high school coach, Ray Dicharry, in 1950 I was offered a football scholarship at Auburn University, then known as Alabama Polytechnic Institute (API).

Football was my main motivation for going to college, but with time I slowly gained an appreciation for learning and became a fairly good student, thanks primarily to that disciplined Catholic school background. I graduated in four years with a degree in business management and was commissioned a second lieutenant in the Marine Corps—all on the same day. I left shortly thereafter to fulfill my two-year active duty obligations. I enjoyed the Corps and might have stayed in had I not had an offer by my API head coach, Ralph "Shug" Jordan, to return to my alma mater as an assistant coach. Even then I stayed in the Marine Reserves the entire time I was an assistant coach. Each summer I would attend two weeks of camp at various U.S. Marine bases.

During my eight years as an assistant coach at Auburn I began to experience a real joy for learning. The GI Bill was a big incentive for me to take advantage of some down time after football season to enroll in history courses, a subject I always enjoyed in school. I took so many courses that I eventually qualified to enroll in graduate school, and after almost eight years received my master's degree. The process was a good example of persistence motivated by an enjoyable journey.

As an aside, the time span provided two degrees from the same school. However, the advanced degree took me so long that I received a bachelor of science in business from Alabama Polytechnic Institute in 1954 and a master of art in history from Auburn University in 1963.

Shortly after receiving my master's, to the utter shock of the entire Bulldog Nation, I became Georgia's head coach. Little did I know, at age thirty-one, how poorly prepared I was at the time. Thankfully, ignorance is bliss. Looking back I have come to realize only three people thought it was a good hire: the athletic director, Joel Eaves, who hired me; my wife, Barbara; and me! Nevertheless, with some good players and coaches, and good fortune, I acquired temporary security by winning two SEC championships the first five years. This allowed me to start satisfying my newly acquired joy of learning. I started auditing courses in history, especially those on warfare, leadership, and politics that I found helpful in my job as football coach. Auditing instead of enrolling was a good fit for the time constraints of my job. My classroom educational pursuit was augmented by traveling each summer with Barbara and our friends Myrna and Loran Smith leading Georgia Bulldog groups to countries around the world. It was a great opportunity to not only read but walk in the footsteps of history. We traveled to most countries in Europe and in the Far and Middle East, as well as North Africa and South America. We visited most every major art museum in the world, which then prompted me to audit courses in art history.

During many of those trips we also visited gardens around the world, but ironically I was never moved to take full advantage of those opportunities. I regret that today. Only the breathtaking beauty of the Italian gardens of Villa d'Estes at Tivoli made a lasting impression on me. That remembrance was due more to the gardens' Renaissance historical significance and the incredible age-old technology that gave life to the magical fountains in the gardens. It certainly wasn't the shrubs and trees that caught my attention. The horticulture bug hadn't hit yet, and I suppose my lack of interest reflected the fact that I had absolutely no prior background in plants or gardening growing up in a modest neighborhood in downtown Mobile, Alabama. Although my parents were not gardeners, I remember distinctly the beautiful blue bigleaf hydrangea in our front yard. On refection, it might have been an omen of things to come.

Those beautiful blue flowers were always in bloom during the month of May. That was timely since that month was dedicated to the Virgin Mary by the Catholic

My mentors in horticulture have been Michael Dirr and Allan Armitage (right photo).

Church, and we used the flowers to each day crown Mary's statue in the Cathedral grammar school yard. Those blue hydrangeas tied to a wire frame made a beautiful crown, and I have great memories of climbing the ladder to reach up and adorn the life-sized statue of Mary located in a grotto while the school in assembly sang the chorus of the song "Oh, Mary, We Crown Thee with Blossoms Today."

I recall only one other incident that might have indicated an early horticulture interest. That occurred while I was coaching at Georgia. During the light Monday practices in October after a win the previous weekend, I would pause to take in the environment. Just outside the practice field were three beautiful trees in fall color. The leaves on one turned a magnificent golden yellow, the other a bright red, and the third a brilliant orange, all glowing in the sun. I would pause briefly in admiration and wonder about the names of those majestic specimens. The thought was fleeting, however, as I was soon back focused on practice. I experienced that wonderful horticultural pause on other occasions in the fall, especially when we visited Lexington, Kentucky, every other year to play the Wildcats. I remember reflecting on how magnificent the tree colors were, but

my marine discipline would quickly bring me back to the mission of combat with the Kentucky Wildcats.

THE HORTICULTURE CURIOSITY

Only after giving up coaching in 1989 to devote myself full time as athletic director did I feel I decide to satisfy my new horticultural curiosity. My plan was to take one survey course on shrub and tree identification and, thus satisfied, move on to something else. Little did I know what I was getting into when the instructor for that course happened to be an enthusiastic professor named Dr. Michael Dirr. Little did I know at the time that Dr. Dirr was known nationally and internationally as the guru of woody shrubs and trees. I also didn't know that Dr. Dirr had written the Bible for that subject, *Manual of Woody Landscape Plants*, a three-inch-thick book that would eventually become one of my best friends throughout my journey. At the time Dr. Dirr had just completed his fourth edition of the book and would go on to write a total of thirteen books (so far)! What I really didn't know was how this passionate, enthusiastic teacher would launch me on a pursuit of horticultural

Horticulture class in the field

learning that has not been satisfied even today. I probably became infected. Barbara, a little more expressive, said, "I didn't know Michael Dirr would inhabit his body!"

To make matters worse, or rather better, I should say, the university had not only one of the most respected horticulture teachers in the country but two. The other was Allan Armitage, who, like Dirr, is a horticulture guru, whose specialty is herbaceous plants. Armitage has written the bible on the subject entitled *Herbaceous Perennial Plants*, not to mention eleven other books on perennial and annual plants. He is equipped with the same passion as Dirr, and both are magnificent teachers.

I ended up auditing five courses under Dirr and three under Armitage. As you can imagine, the students truly enjoy their classes under these two dynamic instructors. Good teachers do make going to school fun. That first course under Dirr was a challenge and more than I had bargained for. He insisted that the students learn the botanical names of the plants and then the common name. Remembering the Latin name was one ordeal; pronouncing them was another. The struggle did eventually pay off, and today I still recall the botanical names most often

before the common. However, people accuse me of speaking "southern Latin" when using the botanical names! Besides the botanical name challenge, Dirr was a rapid-fire professor, and this neophyte had a hard time listening and keeping up with what he said. The students, most of them "hort" majors, were used to Professor Dirr, so I was really on a horticulture island. I found a way, however, when I started making friends and sitting next to Dr. Waddell Barnes of Macon, Georgia, who was also auditing the class. He was well schooled in Latin with his medical background. I spent most of the semester either asking, "What did he say?" or simply copying his notes. Dr. Barnes was a godsend getting me through my first course, while I adjusted to the botanical names from the fast-talking professor. Incidentally, the Macon State Botanical Garden is named in honor of Dr. Barnes, who was instrumental in establishing that fine garden for the school.

While I enjoyed the class work, even more fun was taking campus walks and seeing the shrubs and trees come alive. For every two class dates, there was a least one campus walk, or in a lot of cases, such as in Armitage's class, visits to noted gardens in the city.

Both Dirr and Armitage gave exams on the class lectures and class walks or outdoor lab portion. This is where I had the advantage. I didn't have to take the exams. I have said many times that auditing classes is the ideal way to attend school for a senior citizen who has "been there and done that." So I would sit in the class, enjoy the lectures, take notes, do research, and when the exams came, get up and wish the students the best and with a salute say, "Good luck! I will see you in class tomorrow."

Dirr and Armitage were both generous about giving me plants, and before long I ended up with a group of plants, yet unsure of what to do with them. I had never gardened in my life. Not only did I not know where the plants should go, but I didn't even know how to plant them. I needed some help but I didn't want to let my teachers know what a greenhorn gardener I was, so I grabbed a shovel and a plant and began to learn how to create my first garden.

As a focused football coach I left practically every decision to Barbara both in the house and in the yard. In the house Barbara had domestic help with Daisy Mitchell who came twice a week. The yard work was done by Henry Cleveland who came by once a week. Barbara had little interest in the garden, so Henry was virtually the master of the yard. Barbara would occasionally buy plants and Henry would plant them. One such plant became somewhat famous thirty years later. Barbara, always looking for a bargain, in keeping with her Lebanese heritage, found a nursery owned by George Upchurch going out of business in 1968, so she got a deal on three bigleaf hydrangeas (*Hydrangea macrophylla*). Henry planted them next to the house and there they remained for twenty-five years, showing off their billowy flowers until Dirr came along and finally named them the 'Dooley' hydrangea—a story for a later chapter.

The only other time Barbara showed any interest in the garden was when our youngest child, Derek, was five years old and wanted a vegetable garden of everything he liked. As the three older children, Deanna, Daniel, and Denise, used to say, whatever "precious" wanted, "precious" got. Henry orchestrated the planting with Barbara and baby Derek bonding, especially during the harvest.

I got my basic garden training from Henry, but that might not have been the case without some divine intervention. Henry was a very religious man and started working for Barbara after he appeared at our door in his standard overalls, stating that the Lord told him she needed

Hydrangea macrophylla 'Dooley'
Bigleaf Hydrangea

him to work in her garden. Barbara, who also listens attentively to the Lord, hired Henry on the spot. She grew to love Henry especially so as he always brought her cut flowers, which made her happy. The ol' saying goes, "When Mama is happy, everybody is happy," and I was happy Henry was keeping Barbara happy!

When I was offered an opportunity to return to my alma mater, Auburn, to coach, Henry told me that the Lord told him I should go. Being one who is dubious about getting a message from the Lord indirectly from a gardener, I decided to stay at Georgia. Henry, confident that I was going, came to the press conference where I would announce my decision. He was dressed to the nines in his three-piece suit, sporting his gold pocket watch and chain. After I announced I was staying at Georgia, Henry quit, telling Barbara he "ain't working for no man who don't listen to the Lord!"

Barbara tried other gardeners but missed old Henry. One day, five years later, she saw him working in a neighbor's yard and she stopped and told him the Lord had told her to tell him to come back and work in our garden. Henry, who always listens to the Lord, especially through

a passionate messenger like Barbara, returned to our garden. By this time Henry was getting older and spent more time philosophizing about gardening than working the soil, but he kept Barbara happy with flowers and conversations over coffee.

When I started my garden interests, Henry and I had some great times together, and he taught me a lot of things, including a unique propagation technique that fascinated Dr. Dirr. Henry used to laugh at those college gardeners who got their knowledge, as he used to say, from a book. Henry, to Dirr's amazement, rooted hydrangeas using a modified laying technique that was highly successful. It consisted of cutting the branches about an arm's length from the hydrangea, laying them in a three-inch-deep trench, and covering them up. From each of the nodes on the stems a hydrangea shoot will sprout up. Today there is a grouping of hydrangeas in the garden attributed to Henry's layering techniques.

As Henry slowed down physically, I began to hit my gardening stride, and the increased workload I gave Henry, coupled with me slowly taking control of his domain, prompted him to tell me that the Lord told him it was time to retire. Henry is in an assisted living home today. Occasionally he comes by for a cup of coffee and reminisces and expounds on his garden philosophy. I will always be indebted to Henry for giving me my basic gardening training. The following are a few basic Henry fundamentals that have proven to be sound in my horticulture journey. Henry strongly believed in that old 4-H club motto "Learn by doing" and I believe strongly in the adage "Experience is the best teacher." Henry was also a great believer in soil preparation. He always told me I needed to do my own composting, so after a while I purchased a compost barrel that I still use today to turn leaves and food waste. Third, Henry always said, "If a plant ain't happy, move 'em!" I have moved a lot of them during my journey.

With some book learning and some practical gardening experience from Henry, I was now ready to enhance the garden. I needed a consultant and Ron Deal, a landscape designer, appeared on the scene. I had acquired some more plants and wanted advice on placement and garden design. Ron appeared to be the right man at the right hour. I was excited and told Barbara about him, and she shouted, "Who??" I said answered, "Ron Deal," and she bellowed, "Ron Deal!? I fired him last year!" Turns out that Barbara had fired Ron after Henry Cleveland quit when I didn't "listen to the Lord" and turned down the Auburn job. Nobody pleased Barbara after Henry, including a few other aspiring garden workers. Apparently none of them, including Ron, understood that part of the gardening qualification was good yard work plus good social conversation skills like Henry. Ron is much wiser now. The first thing he does when he arrives for work is come in the house to drink coffee and converse with Barbara before heading to the garden. Ron bills by the hour and always includes the social hours, marked as consulting!

Ron has worked with me now for over a decade, and he and his wife, Nan, and lovely daughter, Laura, have become good friends. He is talented, confident, and has a good eye. On the other hand, every now and then he reaches a little higher, as evidenced by his many attempts at building a water feature. He could write a book on how not to build and maintain a pond, but he never lacked the confidence to keep trying, and to his credit it now works.

Ron is intelligent and has become a real leader in organizing political action work in Athens to respond to a recent water-restriction crisis that could have been devastating to the industry. To be a good leader like Ron requires promoting, marketing, and the ability to use political spin effectively.

Prunus mume 'Dawn'
Japanese Apricot

The latter experience has helped Ron in his business, and I have witnessed firsthand his use of horticultural spin. Ron loves plants, trees, and flowers, and at the nursery shows he is always on the lookout for something new for my garden. He came back from one show as excited as I have ever seen him, describing this "beautiful flowering apricot [*Prunus mume*] tree covered with these gorgeous double-pink blooms before the leaves emerge." He got me one and I could not wait until bloom time, which takes place interestingly in late January. When it finally bloomed the flowers opened *white*. I challenged Ron about the tree that was supposed to have pink blooms. He calmly said "Oh, white-flowered trees are much preferred over the pink." Incidentally I have since gotten a pink one called 'Dawn' and the weeping light pink, 'W. B. Clark'. I am on the lookout for more. They do provide a gorgeous garden splash in the wintertime.

THE HORTICULTURE BUG

Ron and I have some good times together talking plants and discussing my aspirations for the garden. He has given me some great ideas, and I have increasingly come up with many of my own. Ron placated me early on when I was "bit by the horticulture bug." He didn't say it at the time, but despite my basic training he thought I was as raw a gardener as he had ever seen. I admit early on I was gardening ignorant and reckless. I don't know how many times I called him after breaking water pipes and irrigation lines and cutting outdoor lighting wires. He would patiently come and repair the damage. My horticultural itch was spreading.

Besides Ron, Dirr and Armitage also enjoyed seeing me acquire this horticulture bug. As teachers they constantly fed my newfound passion. This horticulture itch started in my head, spread to my hands, and then to my heart. I was like a little baby exploring everything and finding something new every day. I once told Barbara I used to drive around the Georgia campus enjoying looking at the pretty girls, but now I find myself looking at trees and shrubs. She was happy, of course, but reminded me the scenery-change preference on campus might come with age! Perhaps, but I rather think that while I still enjoy the natural coed beauty of the campus, my vision is now more diverse. For sure, it is great fun to see new plants and trees blooming and immediately start researching to find out what they are. It is always satisfying to find the answer.

In addition to Dirr's and Armitage's books, I perused other plant books, discovering new plants I had to have. I soon developed my first, though rather ridiculous, gardening philosophy. Simply put, it was to get one of every plant! I gave it a good try before I succumbed to the obvious—it was impossible to do—but I am still trying. The effort has given me great variety in my garden.

With study, experience, and maturity, I learned the basics of planting different varieties of trees and shrubs, also the basic arrangements of planting in threes and fives and planting small in front and tall in back. I also learned

Pinus densiflora 'Oculus-Draconis'
Dragon Eye Japanese Red Pine

important knowledge about growth habits. I would plant an area and it would look harmonious and wonderful at first. If only the plants had stayed in their places, but they do grow and invade each other's territory. Learning growth habits was helpful, but more important was learning that plants can be moved. I have in a dozen or so years moved hundreds of plants and trees around my garden, and most survived after I learned when, where, and how to move them. I was constantly jumping at learning opportunities and enrolled in a master gardening course. I eventually graduated with a Master Gardener's certificate but felt like I only scratched the surface and probably should have repeated the course.

To expand my knowledge I started reading, for the first time ever, the garden section of the newspapers. Early on the *Atlanta Journal Constitution* had some excellent garden writers in Walter Reeves, Lee May, Erica Glasener, and Martha Tate. My sister, Rosezella Zakrzewski, who always sent me clippings from my hometown newspaper, the *Mobile Press Register*, started sending me articles by Bill Finch, a talented horticulture and environmental editor. Unfortunately, with the decline of the newspaper, garden sections have been severely cut. I also subscribed to several horticulture magazines to quench my newfound thirst. Today, with the Internet I can get instant satisfaction of any horticultural curiosity, thanks to my assistant Julie Taylor, a young technology wiz, and/or Barbara, who has developed good computer skills.

In Georgia, Erica Glasener and Walter Reeves have been at the forefront of reaching out to the gardening public in the print media and on the radio and television. They coauthored five books on Georgia plants. While I was still very wet behind the ears, Erica had me on her *Gardener's Diary* TV show and presented to me afterward a rare Dragon Eye Japanese red pine (*Pinus densiflora* 'Oculus-Draconis'). I still have one today.

Walter is an icon in the gardening world in Georgia. He is extremely knowledgeable on every phase of gardening, and his pleasing and patient personality is perfect for his ultra successful three-hour gardening show every Saturday morning on WSB Atlanta. I listen to it when I can.

Another of his faithful followers is my friend Dan Cathy, president of Chick-fil-A and son of Truett, the founder. Dan has also been horticulturally infected, of which we both know there is no antidote. We have become good friends and visited each other's gardens, though Dan's is in another league. Because of his busy schedule with Chick-fil-A, he seizes opportunities instantly and has the capacity to do so in large quantities. I picked up four Japanese maples (all my car could hold) at a bargain price in Commerce, Georgia. The store, with a huge inventory, was going out of business so my intention was to return for more bargains. Barbara told Dan about the sale, and in grand scale he sent two flatbed trucks up and bought the entire inventory. Though in fairness to Dan, who is a superb businessman, a good part of his horticulture mission is to aid in landscaping the many Chick-fil-A stores around the country. He has developed a magnificent garden from scratch in his Fayetteville, Georgia, home. His wife, Rhonda, like Barbara, thinks we both have gone off the "horticulture deep end."

The latest tip I picked up from listening to Walter Reeves's radio show is to constantly check the irrigation system during the summer months. I have quite an extensive system (though nothing compared to Dan Cathy's) and I now check each of the many stations every two weeks, and always discover some malfunction. This diligence has saved the lives of many plants.

Walter mentioned often on his show the value of rain barrels but it never made a lasting impression until our area went through near devastating droughts in 2006, 2007, and 2008. The crisis resulted in a no-water-usage restriction that really got my attention. Today I have several rain barrels in the patio that are very helpful especially in watering the many potted plants I acquired in the area.

Still the journey continued . . .

CHAPTER TWO

THE UNIVERSITY OF GEORGIA CAMPUS ARBORETUM

THE URBAN TREE ADVISORY COMMITTEE

*W*ord was beginning to spread around the community that I had become interested in horticulture and gardening. As a result I was asked to serve on various committees, foremost being the Athens Urban Tree Advisory Committee. I wasn't sure at the time what the committee was all about, but it sounded like another opportunity to learn more about my newfound interest, so I accepted and became a member in 1998.

At the first meeting, I had that old neophyte feeling again and wondered, "What in the heck am I doing here?" The chair was Hal Cofer Jr. who owned Cofer's Home and Garden Center. On the committee were four foresters, a retired horticulturist, a landscape architect, a UGA art professor, the municipal landscape manager of Athens-Clarke County, and me—a retired football coach. We immediately went on a two-day retreat with the goal of forming a strategic plan. I wasn't sure what the group was talking about most of the time, but I was a willing participant anxious to make some kind of contribution.

My opportunity came at the next meeting when our chair was reading out potential committees and project assignments. I didn't understand any of

Ulmus americana
American Elm

the projects recited until "UGA as an arboretum" was mentioned. I knew that was my only chance to serve, so I immediately threw my hand up and was given the assignment.

I knew a little about the subject after reading two newspaper articles that featured Dr. Dirr expounding on the value of the campus being an arboretum and then asking the question: Why would anybody be against that?

I soon found out that nobody was against the campus being an arboretum, but in order to do anything at a university there is a process that takes time, which went against Dirr's frequently stated "We are wasting time" philosophy.

While I didn't know much about an arboretum campus, from my years of coaching I did know something about putting a team together and organizing them to be productive.

I recruited an arboretum committee class comparable to my best football recruiting class of 1979, which featured two consensus All-Americans—Herschel Walker and Terry Hoag—and many more dedicated and talented players. That class won a national championship (1980), three SEC championships (1980, '81, '82), and had a four-year record of 43-4-1, the best in the nation during that span of time. Dirr was the Herschel Walker of my arboretum committee, but he had an incredible supporting cast, just like Herschel did.

The committee consisted of nine renowned professors at the university: two in forestry, four in horticulture, two in botany, and one in environmental design. In addition there was the head of the grounds department and the director of campus planning at the university, as well as two regional directors of the United States Forestry Service. This was the top arboretum recruiting class in the country, and of all things, I was the chair. My job was to simply set the meetings, open the discussion, keep it focused, and get out of the way!

It is hard to single out one committee member over another, but to give you a flavor of the talent I will mention just a few. Kim Coder, forestry professor and internationally recognized expert on trees, was a committee member, along with Allan Armitage, known throughout the world as an expert on annuals and perennials. Dirr, also known internationally as a woody plant and tree expert, really carried the ball but did get good help from Dexter Adams, head of the university's grounds department, and Ingrid Sather, technical service coordinator of the United States Forestry Service.

Despite the individual talent on the committee, they worked well together in defining the mission of the arboretum, outlining the goals and steering the project through the necessary university processes. And it was quite a process!

CAMPUS ARBORETUM STUDIES

Since I volunteered to chair this project I felt compelled to become a little more knowledgeable about campus arboretums. Fortunately, prior to calling the first committee meeting, I was able to visit two of the best campus arboretums in the country. One campus trip resulted from an NCAA audit invite. I was assigned as part of the NCAA audit team to study the academic athletic compliance programs at the University of Indiana at Bloomington. Ironically, the basketball coach at the time was the infamous Bobby Knight, and the president was the later NCAA president, the late Myles Brand. I was not surprised, incidentally, when a few years later President Brand fired Coach Knight, which of course, ignited quite a controversy. Nevertheless, the three-day audit allowed me plenty of time to visit and explore the Indiana campus. I discovered that Indiana University had a long history of studying and enjoying trees and plants.

It was especially interesting for me to learn that the current arboretum center on campus was the original site of the Indiana Memorial Football Stadium. In 1982 it became necessary to demolish the old stadium. It had been used for football until the late 1950s and for bicycle racing until 1980.

When the space became available, there was a political clamor for the land's use for either a parking garage or an academic building. Instead the administration wisely chose to dedicate the area to the preservation of diverse plants, since the campus, as so many others, had lost its pastoral quality to academic and athletic programs. Campus green space at Indiana was a decade ahead of Georgia, which started "green theme" planning at the turn of the century.

I was especially impressed that the Indiana University administration decided that while creating a beautiful green space for the campus they also wanted to create an architectural link with the past by maintaining the features of the old stadium. The old ticket booths and stadium entrance were very effectively used in the arboretum.

The university's arboretum area was roughly eleven acres, with a stream running down the middle. Some of the old trees that had long surrounded the stadium were retained, while many new dedicatory trees have been planted throughout the arboretum.

The beauty of the arboretum setting is best captured by then-president John Ryan at a 1982 alumni dinner: "It will be a place where students can find wooded tranquility and where alumni can recapture the sense of something dear

Liriodendron tulipifera
Tulip Poplar

gone by; a place of serenity and beauty that will refresh the spirits of those who come to us seeking knowledge."

I also had the privilege of visiting the Scott Arboretum on the Swarthmore College campus in eastern Pennsylvania, whose history dates back to 1929. An estimated 3,000 different kinds of plants and trees grow on the 300-acre campus, and I did my best in a limited three-hour span to visit all of them, at times jogging from one to the other. This quaint college town close to Philadelphia has a magnificent arboretum that is on my bucket list to revisit.

After visiting and studying the campus arboretum at the University of Indiana at Bloomington and Swarthmore I felt more confident about chairing our talented and learned group who volunteered their valuable time to make the University of Georgia a campus arboretum.

COMMITTEE MEETINGS

At the first meeting we decided to draft a mission statement, and Dr. Dirr responded by authoring a splendid piece setting forth the purpose of the campus arboretum. In essence the arboretum was to provide a "biological and aesthetic collection of trees, shrubs, and herbaceous plants in a designed setting for the enjoyment and education of the students, faculty, staff, and citizens of Georgia." In addition the purpose was "to map, label, and otherwise promote the extant and future tree and shrub collections." The mission statement also pointed out that the University of Georgia campus is "recognized nationally as one of the best planted and maintained, and from a teaching standpoint the tremendous woody plant diversity serves classes in botany, forestry, ecology, horticulture, and landscape architecture." In addition, "art and photography utilize the campus as a natural extension of the classroom."

I acquired a special appreciation for the beauty of the Georgia campus after receiving a copy of a letter sent from noted horticulturist and Auburn professor Dr. Ken Tilt to President Michael Adams in 2001. Dr. Tilt wanted President Adams to know the "arboretum treasure" that he, the faculty, and the students had inherited. Dr. Tilt called it "an academic and cultural jewel as important as your new museum and performing arts theater." Dr. Tilt further stated that he had been on many campus planning committees in the past decade and said that "when the members were asked what they would like their city or campus to look like . . . they responded UNC Chapel Hill or UGA Athens." What a compliment! It sure stirred my campus community pride.

Over the next several meetings the committee made rapid strides toward its goal, with several new initiatives that were planned or implemented. Dexter Adams of campus planning arranged for all trees on campus to be mapped and labeled. A campus tree walk brochure was planned. The Georgia Power Company then committed $10,000 for the publication and the labeling. Melwood Springs and the Georgia Athletic Association donated additional funds to complete the projects. However, the toughest job ahead was to maneuver through the university process for approval.

It started with the Faculty Facilities Committee, and I persuaded Dirr to appear in a coat and tie to make his presentation. Dirr putting a coat and tie on a body that traditionally wears shorts, tennis shoes, sport shirt, and Bulldog cap was the ultimate sacrifice for the cause. Next came the approval of the University Council Executive Committee, which was more challenging because it was necessary to devise a management scheme that would ensure the continuation of the arboretum in the future. This objective started with me planning to pass the torch to the head of the horticulture department as soon as the arboretum was up and running. Following the approval of the executive committee, the full council approved the project, and finally President Michael Adams gave his endorsement. We concluded with a dedication ceremony on campus. The whole process took one and a half years from the time I first formed the committee. It was a typical university process, which in the long run was a good thing, building consensus and leaving no stone unturned.

The Georgia campus arboretum is a point of pride for all those who served to make it happen. This was especially true of Dirr, who with his boundless energy labeled the trees and wrote the brochure for the campus arboretum walking tour of trees.

The brochure, still in existence today, guides tours of three campus walks: the north, central, and south campus. The north campus (0.5 miles) starts at the Arch on Broad Street, goes to the library, and returns—covering forty-five labeled trees, each described in the brochure. The central walk (1.7 miles) starts at Memorial Hall next to the stadium and winds by the chemistry and physics building—covering forty-nine trees, each numbered corresponding to the tree description. The south campus walk (2.5 miles) starts at Conner Hall on Cedar Street, opens up into the trial garden at UGA, and winds down to the tennis courts—consisting of sixty trees. All three walks bring the grand total to 154 labeled trees on the entire campus tour.

CHAPTER THREE

ART AND HISTORY

ART AND HISTORY

My passionate pursuit of plants soon led me to further explore other topics that were horticulturally related that I also enjoyed, such as art and history. When I had earlier audited courses in art history to better understand the work of some of the great masters we visited in the classic museums around the world, I became a fan of impressionist painters. I soon learned in my horticulture journey that most of them were avid gardeners. On a trip to England and France in 1995 with my son Derek and my first grandson, Patrick Dooley Cook, we retraced the D-Day invasion at Normandy. While doing so we spent a good day at Giverny, the site of Monet's house and garden. I had been there before but never appreciated it as I did this time. I later was given a wonderful book by my Athens friend and talented artistic gardener Mary Hardman entitled *The Impressionist Garden*, by Derek Fell, which treats some of the great impressionist painters as gardeners. What got my attention was that the two great masters, Monet and Renoir, both avid gardeners, had completely different attitudes on gardening. Monet was described as having "a high orchestrated effect" and that his garden was consistently under control with repeated pruning. Renoir was the antithesis of Monet, letting nature have a free hand, not pruning or weeding much at all. Monet once said, "My only two interests in life were painting and gardening."

My garden history interest was initially restricted to learning about happenings in Athens and the university. Athens, known as the Classic City, has a rich garden history. The first garden club of America was founded in the Classic City in January of 1891. Today, on the campus, the delightful two-and-a-half-acre Founder's Memorial Garden is dedicated to the twelve women who formed and organized the first ladies garden club. An advisor to the women and strong advocate of the club was Dr. Edward D. Newton, a horticulturist of wide repute. Athens historian Charlotte Marshall once showed me Newton's grave site in the Oconee Hill Cemetery across from the stadium. Inscribed on the tombstone are these simple but significant words: "Edward D. Newton, Surgeon in Lee's Army 1861–1865; Founder of First Ladies Garden Club in America."

Dr. Newton served as a surgeon in General Lee's Army of Northern Virginia, and as quoted in his private journal he "enjoyed the personal acquaintance and friendship of the South's greatest commander whose memory he revered." Few people know that Newton helped organize the first women's garden club, not only for his great interest in horticulture but because he was also interested in finding some socially accepted exercise for women. He felt that many of the women's health problems he was encountering at the time were caused by poor muscle tone and circulation. In that era women wore tightly fitted garments and multiple petticoats, so both fashion and social customs encouraged little mobility. Gardening was Newton's way of getting women to perform socially accepted exercise while enjoying a wonderful hobby.

A unique piece of horticulture trivia about Athens is that the Classic City is the only site in the world with a tree that "owns itself." Not long ago the Junior Ladies Club of Athens celebrated the fiftieth birthday of the tree that owns itself. The speaker for the occasion was my good friend, legendary former university tennis coach and Master Gardener, the one and only Dan Magill. Coach Magill, a delightful humorist, started his speech proclaiming that "Paris has its Eiffel Tower; Rome, its Coliseum; India, its Taj Mahal; China, its Great Wall; New York, its Empire State Building; and San Francisco, its Golden Gate . . . and Athens, Georgia, has 'the tree that owns itself!'" He said that while those great cities around the world have incredible massive structures, the Classic City's landmark is "unique among great cities because it is a living, breathing monument which majestically changes with the season and grows in stature and beauty annually."

This massive white oak (*Quercus alba*) is located on Finley Street. When they cut the street originally, plans called for it to go through the tree's plot, but it so outraged the citizenry at the time that their vocal outcry caused the street to be detoured around the land on which the tree stands. An appropriate plaque dedicated in 1988 describes its history.

THE TREE THAT OWNS ITSELF
Quercus alba

Deeded to itself by Col. William H. Jackson
Circa 1832
This scion of the original tree was planted by
the Junior Ladies Garden Club in 1946

National Register of Historic Plants 1975
Athens Historical Landmark 1988

Next to the plaque inserted on a concrete marker is the original grant to the tree by Col. Jackson:

"For and in consideration of the great love I bear this tree and the great desire I have for its protections for all time. I convey entire possession of itself and all land within eight feet of the tree on all sides."

WILLIAM H. JACKSON

Another bit of Georgia horticulture history occurred in the southeastern part of the state. The Franklin tree (*Franklinia alatamaha*) was discovered by the famous botanist John Bartram in 1765 on the Altamaha River around Darien while exploring the southern coastal region with his son, William. They named the tree after their revered friend Ben Franklin. This small tree, which is no longer found in the wild, has beautiful cupped white fragrant flowers. The tree has never been found anywhere else in the world; and thanks to the Bartrams, who on their explorations to the South collected seeds from this plant, all Franklinias today are direct descendants from the seeds and plants collected by the Bartrams in the eighteenth century. For many years horticulture historians thought that the *Franklinia* was a native plant, but another theory is that it was introduced by early colonists searching for a substitute for tea. I have had several *Franklinias*, trying to disprove that it does not do well in the South, but after I lost my third and last one, I am a believer!

ADAMS AND JEFFERSON

One of the most interesting horticulture and history ties I discovered came while reading David McCullough's *John Adams*. At the turn of the nineteenth century Adams and Thomas Jefferson became bitter enemies during their rival bid for the presidency. However, before the rivalry, with common interest in gardening, both bonded in the gardens of England in the spring of 1784.

Adams was then Minister to England and Jefferson was Minister to France. Both were in London together negotiating with the Barbary pirates to open trade routes. They took a break, hired a coach, and took off on a tour of gardens in the countryside.

Jefferson had a copy of Thomas Whately's *Observations on Modern Gardening* that they used as a guide. They traveled along the Thames and found "cool mornings as they observed cherry blossom in bloom and daffodils in abundant bloom." McCullough described these two Founding Fathers traveling together "free of work or responsibility; both countrymen and farmers interested in the soil."

Whately's guidebook said gardening should "rank among the liberal arts," as he described at the time the modern or new style English landscape gardens. This meant "no regularity and garden arrangements" but "natural arrangements." This was radically different from the highly symmetrical gardens made fashionable by the French at the time.

In five days they had toured about twenty country sites and gardens. One highlight was Stowe, regarded at the time as the most famous garden in England. It comprised some 400 acres with a manor house, lakes, waterfalls, and numerous architectural stops, such as the temples of Victory, Venus, and Bacchus. It was too bad that time and transportation constraints prevented Adams and Jefferson from visiting just seventy-five miles down the road to my favorite landscape garden, Stourhead. The garden is a majestic and enchanted lap around the lake that is lined with noble trees and architectural follies, such as the temples of Flora and Apollo and the magnificent Pantheon. While these two American giants missed the opportunity to lap the lake, today over 3,000 visitors daily stroll and enjoy the garden and the lakeside view of architecture, plants, and trees.

Stourhead Pantheon

After parting ways, these two future American presidents engaged in bitter political struggles for the better part of their lives. But for five days they bonded in their mutual love of the soil and appreciation of the garden as a work of art.

FEATURES IN THE GARDEN

As I continued to learn and grow our garden, the main residence also underwent transformation. Since moving into our house in the summer of 1964, there have been ten major additions. Every time one of our four children would leave for college Barbara wanted to add a room. That didn't make sense until now; they have multiplied, giving us eleven grandchildren that all have a place to stay when they visit.

The last addition, a sunroom provided by my friends Champion Windows of Atlanta, has been the favorite of both Barbara and me, though initially she was very much against it. Barbara loves it now because it is a spiritual sanctuary where she can meditate and say her daily prayers while listening to the rhythmic sound of water cascading in the pond just outside the open window.

While reading Pat Dunleavy's fine book *Landscape Lessons,* I ran across a quote that speaks to the spirituality of waterfalls. Pat runs Pinebush Nursery outside Athens with her husband, John. She quotes the late Dr. Eugene Odum, "Father of Ecology," for whom the school of ecology at the University of Georgia is named. In his book, *Essence of Place,* Dr. Odum writes, "Waterfalls are musical landscapes, not only beautiful to observe but also pleasant to hear."

Barbara not only listens to the musical landscape of the waterfall but she also lets her eyes wander to two religious statues that are most meaningful to her: Mary the Blessed Virgin and a Celtic cross are both accentuated with lighting at night. Barbara's small Bible study group meets in the sunroom every Monday.

While I share Barbara's appreciation for the spiritual benefits of the glass patio room, I also like it because it brings the garden into the house, or the reverse. It enables me not only to see and enjoy the flowers and shrubs in the garden but to enjoy two of my favorite bronze children statues, *Nina* and her brother *Billy.* Young Nina is lying prone next to the pond reading a book, while her brother Billy is fishing on the other side. I have several other

Mary the Blessed Virgin

Celtic Cross

Nina

Billy

bronze children statues throughout the garden that I enjoy, and they often become conversation pieces while giving garden tours.

FENCES AND HEDGES

In addition to plants, shrubs, and trees, I began to study and appreciate other horticultural elements with both artistic and historical significance. Fences and hedges featured in American gardens had their roots in Italian, English, and French gardens of the seventeenth century. Other features such as avenues and groves can be traced back to Persian, Roman, and Greek times. Hedges and fences were used throughout Europe both as ornamentals and utilitarian barriers against livestock.

Still standing today at the University of Georgia in Athens is a classic example of both an ornamental and utilitarian fence. In the antebellum period the university had a botanical garden (1833–54) located just east of the campus and downtown Athens was described as a virtual "Garden of Eden with hills and valleys . . . two brooks, a lake . . . and over 2,000 plants, shrubs, and trees from every corner of the globe." Due to a recession in the early 1850s the university sold the garden for $1,000. The money was used to build a black-iron ornamental fence that surrounded the

entire campus at the time. The primary function of the fence was to serve as a barrier to the livestock that roamed the campus in those days. The historical fence still stands today.

The most famous hedge is in Normandy, France. For centuries these enormous hedges, both tall and thick, were used to defend against the strong Atlantic seacoast winds. The hedgerow gained notoriety during World War II as this formidable natural obstacle was used by the Germans to stymie the American army advance after D-Day. Some of the fiercest fighting of the war took place in the hedgerow as the Allies struggled to clear the hedges of the entrenched German army.

One of the most famous hedges in the United States is right here in Athens, Georgia. They surround the football field of Sanford Stadium and serve as a barrier against excessively celebrating fans after a great victory. It also serves as a battle cry ("We got 'em between the hedges!") for the Georgia Bulldogs when they play at home.

The famed hedges were installed just in time for the dedication game of Sanford Stadium in 1929 when the Georgia Bulldogs hosted the Yale Bulldogs in what was the biggest game held in the South at the time. In 2009 the school celebrated the eightieth birthday of the "most famous flora in all of football, if not all of sports." As John

Ligustrum sinense, The Hedges
Chinese Privet

D. Lukacs, college football historian, points out, the Georgia Bulldog hedge has been in existence "long before the renowned Boston ivy began creeping along the red brick walls of Wrigley Field . . . even before the brilliant blooming rainbow arced across Augusta National."

Of all the shrubs used today as hedges, such as boxwoods, hollies, and viburnums, the hedges of Sanford Stadium are simply common ol' Chinese privet (*Ligustrum sinense*). As common and invasive as it is, it's sacred to Georgia fans! When the "royal hedges" were removed for the medal soccer games of the 1996 Centennial Olympics, it caused great displeasure for all football purists. Cuttings were taken and grown at Dudley's Nursery in Thomson, Georgia, and Hackney's Nursery in Greensboro, Florida, as a backup. When the Olympics were over, the cuttings from Hedges I grew to be "sons and daughters," becoming known as Hedges II in Sanford Stadium today.

Before 1987 my alma mater, Auburn University, never had hedges around their stadium. That changed after a spirited group of Georgia students and fans stormed the field to celebrate a stunning upset victory in 1986. When overly enthusiastic fans started to collect souvenirs from the Auburn turf, the Bulldogs' parade got rained on—literally! Tiger officials turned the water hose on them and later turned the water on the Georgia faithful celebrating in the stands. The infamous water-hose game stirred quite a controversy between these two feuding cousins. An Auburn study committee visited our hedges and recommended installation of a hedge, but not our sacred plant. They were determined to install a hedge that would prevent students and fans from ever storming the field again. Auburn installed two lines of defense. The first was the Japanese barberry (*Berberis thunbergii*), which initially appeared to be a good choice. The plant has first-rate color, durability, and forms an impenetrable thick hedge. The downside is the many thorns located on the stems. The sharp spines are up to an inch long!

I remember seeing the barberry hedge on a trip to Auburn after the 1986 game and thinking it would do some heavy damage to some spirited Auburn or visiting students scaling the hedge after a great victory. I thought it was a disaster waiting to happen. After a few years Auburn wisely took the barberry hedges out and replaced them with dwarf Burford Chinese hollies (*Ilex cornuta* 'Dwarf Burford'), a much wiser choice.

ALLÉES AND GROVES

Tree-lined avenues (allées) can be traced back to the Persians. Avenues in antebellum times in the United States served as ceremonial entrances to mansions, estates, and manor houses. In the South, live oak (*Quercus virginiana*) avenues were used mainly in the coastal rice plantation areas such as St. Simons and Sea Island. Many still stand today as awesome historical ties to the past. The eastern redcedar (*Juniperus virginiana*) and southern magnolia (*Magnolia grandiflora*) were also used to line streets.

P. J. Berckmans, once proprietor of Fruitland Nurseries in Augusta, Georgia, planted the avenue of magnolias lead-

ing to their plantation house. Today the avenue still stands and leads to the same house, now the main building of Augusta National, home of the famed Masters golf tournament. I would be remiss if I did not brag on two of the finest players and young men I ever coached who hold highly responsible positions with Augusta National, Billy Payne (1966, '67, '68), the chairman, and Will Jones (1984, '85, '86, '87), director of business affairs.

The entrance avenue to the Trappist Monastery of the Holy Spirit near Conyers, Georgia, is also lined with an allèe of southern magnolias. The trees were planted soon after the monks arrived in the early 1950s from Gaseminee, Kentucky, to start the monastery in Rockdale County. The avenue serves as a hallowed entrance to this wonderful retreat facility. The closest thing I can muster up as an allèe in my garden is an avenue of white-flowering *Hydrangea paniculata* on the upper ridge of the Mathis garden, which are in full glory in late July and August.

Groves, one of the oldest forms of garden art, date back to the Greeks and Romans. It was a natural style of landscape design that helped preserve the forest while providing a shady and pleasant area to assemble, socialize, and in modern times to tailgate!

No place in America is the art of tailgating more of a ritual than in "the grove" on the University of Mississippi campus in Oxford, Mississippi. The eleven-acre grove with more than seventy majestic oaks, along with a variety of other specimen trees, became part of the campus in 1848. Described as the "heartbeat of the school," it is a gathering place for graduations, study, reflection, proposals, weddings, and most of all, tailgating. *Sporting News* calls the grove the "Holy Grail of tailgating," and *Sports Illustrated* calls it "the number one tailgating spot in America." This welcome mat of towering oaks is a large part of the lore of Ole Miss.

The art of tailgating is alive and well on the Georgia campus. Campus spirit, barbeque, and "Glory to Old Georgia" reverberate under some of the many old and majestic campus trees. There are a lot of wonderful tailgate spots on the Georgia campus and throughout the country. Up north, in the Big 10 conference, for instance, there is the beautiful Staley Illini Grove on the University of Illinois at Urbana-Champaign campus. However, the Fighting Illini, as well as the students of all the other beautiful campus gathering sites across our country will have to concede that the grove on the Rebel campus in Mississippi is the crème de la crème of tailgating.

The closest thing I have to a grove in my garden are a couple of benches resting under some large pines (*Pinus taeda*) and tulip poplars (*Liriodendron tulipifera*). There is also a huge rock outcropping in the Mathis garden next to a stately white oak (*Quercus alba*). Known as the engagement rock, it is sacred to Sylvia Gibson, owner of the property that I lease, since her late father William Mathis proposed to her mother, the late Jean Mathis, on that rock.

THE BOTANICAL NAMES

When auditing my first class under Dr. Dirr, I discovered we had to learn the botanical names of plants and trees. Looking back, it was not that much of a problem, since as a gardening neophyte there were few plants and trees I knew the common name for anyway. With a little practice I was reciting botanical names with no problem, in my southern Latin. Before long my curious nature started asking questions: Why are plants given certain names, and how did it all get started? So I thought it would be helpful, especially to nonhorticulturists like me who are reading this book, to offer a simple explanation about the use of botanical names.

First of all, botanical names are used by everyone in all countries throughout the world. Thus there is no doubt as to the precise plant being discussed. This system started some 200 years ago when a fellow by the name of Carl Linnaeus, a Swedish botanist, came up with the "two-name system" that applied order to a lot of confusion that existed at the time. Since Latin was the international language of science and scholarship, plants were given Latin names. In the Catholic Church, Latin was used in saying mass throughout the world, so as a young altar boy I was required to learn enough Latin to serve mass, which served me well in learning botanical nomenclature. Today, of course, mass is said in the vernacular of each country.

Before naming plants the first prerequisite is to place them in their proper family. When I think of family, I think of Barbara, who is keen on family—both our immediate clan as well as her related Lebanese cousins, thousands of whom I have acquired kinship through marriage. Each is part of various subfamilies, but all are part of the related Lebanese family. Plant families are the same way, and it is easy to recognize a family reference because most family names end with *aceae*, which means "of the family of," such as Hydrangeaceae, where the plant *Hydrangea* resides along with a few other generic relatives—*Decumaria*, *Dichroa*, and *Schizophragma*. After the family has been identified, the particular plant can be further identified with a name referred to as a genus, which is always capitalized, in this case *Hydrangea*. The plant is further identified by a specific subdivision called a species (always lower case). Thus the genus *Hydrangea* (*hydra* is Latin for water, and they need plenty) is followed by a specific kind of *Hydrangea* such as the species *macrophylla* (*macro* meaning "long or large leaves"). Thus we have the universal two-name (binomial) system created by Linnaeus (*Hydrangea macrophylla*) that everybody in the world knows and uses.

But not so fast! With the passing of time and in the effort to breed finer forms, a third name appears, which denote "varieties" or "cultivars" further defining the plant. In the case of *Hydrangea macrophylla* the cultivar might be Endless Summer® referring to the reblooming quality of the plant. Or 'Dooley', so named by Dr. Dirr because this cold-hardy plant was discovered in my garden. A few more examples will be helpful. Genus names are Latinized, revealing certain characteristics—like hydro/water—or to commemorate a person or geographic location. For instance, as mentioned previously, the plant *Franklinia alatamaha* was found and named by the exploring botanist John Bartram after his friend Ben Franklin. Discovered on the Altamaha River in southeast Georgia, the plant's species became *alatamaha*, named after the river but with a different spelling for some reason. Species names can also give clues regarding the plant, such as color, size, shape, and habit. Another example is the *Camellia*, named for Father Georg Josep Kamel (1661–1706), a Jesuit priest who wrote an account of the plant in the Philippines. The species may be *japonica*, which refers to "from Japan," and the cultivar may be 'Betty Sanders', in honor of the wife of former Georgia governor and football letterman Carl Sanders. The list goes on and on, as hundreds of thousands of plants have been given botanical names.

Learning to pronounce the names requires some basic rules, however, diction should not be taken too seriously. As I earlier mentioned, my accent causes me to speak southern Latin. However, a few simple emphasis rules have been helpful to me. In two-syllable words the emphasis falls on the first syllable, such as *Acer* (*AC-cer*), a Latin name for maple tree. If the word has three syllables, the emphasis usually is on the middle syllable such as *Forsythia* (*for-SITH-ia*) in honor of William Forsyth, an eighteenth-century author and Scottish superintendent of the Royal Gardens of Kensington Place. Another example is *mag-NO-lia* named for Pierre

Magnol, director of the botanic garden in Montpellier, France, who died in 1751. We can use the species, *M. grandiflora*, meaning "large or showy," describing our southern magnolia and its large white flowers and leaves. If the word has more than three syllables, the emphasis is on the next to the last syllable. Such as (*rho-do-DEN-dron*) meaning "rose tree."

Researching plant names is a lot of fun, and there are two excellent sources on the subject. The first is by Liberty Hyde Bailey, plantsman and botanist extraordinaire, entitled *How Plants Get Their Names*; the other is by the late A.W. Smith entitled *Plant Names: A Gardener's Handbook of Their Meaning and Origins*. Both aid in this horticulture journey of learning. However, if all this is a little too complicated, use the "Armitage system." As he tells his students, "Get the syllables in the right order and fire away!"

CHAPTER FOUR

A WORLD OF GARDENS

STUDIES ABROAD

One of the really exciting opportunities for college students these days is studies abroad. Practically every university and college in the nation has at least one, but most offer a wide variety of such programs. The University of Georgia, for instance, has a hundred studies abroad and exchange programs in fifty-five different countries including Antarctica. There are UGA campuses located in Cortona, Italy; Oxford, England; and San Luis, Costa Rica. These are the only UGA campuses that offer year-round courses and have dormitories on site.

We had the privilege of seeing the program in Cortona firsthand a few summers ago when we rented a villa and took all our children, their spouses, and seven of our eleven grandchildren who were old enough to make the trip. It was a wild adventure to say the least. As we toured the fascinating Tuscany region, we took a couple of days in Cortona to visit the UGA campus, have dinner with the students and faculty, and to say a few words about what was happening in Athens Town and the outlook for the upcoming football season. The next day Rick Johnson, the very capable director of the program, took us to each of their seven different classes to interact with the students. Most of the

Magnolia campbellii
Sino-Himalayan Magnolia

classes were art related but there were classes in Italian and landscape architecture as well. I would love to spend a summer in Cortona taking classes. Cortona, of course, got national attention when the best-selling novel *Under the Tuscan Sun* written by Frances Mayes was made into a popular movie.

This was a return trip to Cortona for Barbara and me. Our first trip abroad to Europe in 1977 was to Italy, and our good friend Dr. Jack Kehoe, who started the program some thirty-eight years ago, talked our tour bus into stopping for a visit. We had a blast visiting this wonderful, old, walled Etruscan city and enjoying some of the region's great wines. The stop was all too short. It was great fun to finally revisit with our family and spend some quality time with Dr. Kehoe and his wife, Marilyn, soaking in all the region has to offer and witnessing the growth of this marvelous studies abroad program that Dr. Kehoe pioneered.

Today it is recognized as one of the most prestigious, successful, and long-lasting American university programs in the entire world.

Meanwhile, my horticulture itch was expanding to what amounted to my own studies abroad program. I was getting the bug just as I took one of my last trips abroad in 1997 with Barbara. I found myself paying as much attention to trees and plants as I was to the historical sites. There were so many I could not identify that I started collecting leaves for future identification. Ironically, on the flight back to Atlanta we were on the same airplane with Dr. Armitage and Dr. Dirr, who were returning from a two-week garden trip to Europe they traditionally led each summer. After a brief hello I seized the opportunity to pull out my leaves for identification. I made up my mind at that moment that my next trip to Europe was going to be a studies abroad horticulture trip.

The opportunity came just a few years later when I joined a small group of horticulture enthusiasts headed by Dr. Dirr in March 1998 to southwest England. The mission was to pursue the magnificent Sino-Himalayan *Magnolia campbellii*. This wonderful area in England known as Cornwall is tempered by the Gulf Stream, which causes the temperature to seldom drop below 30 degrees and seldom rise above 80 degrees Fahrenheit. The even climate allows for most of the plants in the world to grow in the area. Our focus, however, was on the *Magnolia campbellii*. They were awesome! Can you imagine flowers eight to ten inches across with twelve to fifteen sepals with the appearance of a huge water lily? Dirr said, "The beauty cannot be described; it must be experienced." He was right and our gang of eight lavished in the experience. In addition to Dr. Dirr there was Mike Hayman (a photographer) and Bob Hill (a columnist), both of the *Louisville Courier Journal*. There was also Paul Cappiello, a noted horticulturist and former Dirr student;

Verbena canadensis 'Homestead Purple'
Verbena

Magnolia campbellii
Sino-Himalayan Magnolia

George Briggs, director of the North Carolina arboretum; Hillary Barber, another former Dirr student and current employee of Bold Spring Nursery; Dr. Dirr; and myself.

In the gardens at Lanhydrock, Caerhays Castle, and Trewithen the group was running around taking pictures throughout the gardens and became mesmerized as we stumbled upon sixty-foot *Magnolia campbellii* in full flower, with the bloom covering the entire tree before the leaves appeared. While I was truly astonished at the sight, Hillary Barber, who accompanied Dirr on one of his first trips to Cornwall, said the enthusiastic professor was so excited seeing the *Magnolia campbellii* in full glory that she saw him at a distance doing push-ups on a hill next to the tree.

Perhaps it was on the same trip that Dirr later wrote in his book that when he and Allan Armitage first visited southwest England and saw the Sino-Himalayan magnolias they thought they "had ascended to Heaven." He said, "Upon returning to reality we realized that it was only a garden. Perhaps the two are equatable."

Unfortunately we can't grow these magnificent specimens in the South, but there are a huge number of deciduous magnolias that can be grown. I have a good variety in my garden, including four of the yellow-flowered hybrids

such as 'Butterflies'; 'Yellow Fever', 'Elizabeth', and the summer-bloomer 'Hot Flash'.

BACK TO ENGLAND

My first trip to the English gardens only whetted my appetite and by the next summer, June 1999, I found myself agreeing to host, along with Dirr and Sherry Loudermilk, the executive director of the Georgia Green Industry Association, a garden tour of England and Wales. We had a superb group of nursery professionals, landscape architects, and horticulture professors to sign up, and I asked Dirr what in the world I was doing here cohosting these horticulture pros. He replied, "They are basically all students that love plants, and they all love football, so enjoy!"

I met some wonderful nursery people like Randy Hefner, George Tindall, and Charlotte LeBlanc. In addition, there were some landscape professionals like Fred Hooks, a plant lover extraordinaire, who has become a good friend sharing a great love of Japanese maples. Fred is now in business with the great Don Shadow, one of the most respected nurserymen in the business. (Their new business is All Things Acer.) Professor Jim Midcap, expert

Sissinghurst, White Border

Hillier, *Cercis siliquastrum* 'Bodnant'
European Redbud

Hillier, Conifer Collection

horticulturist, was also on the trip—just to name a few of Dirr's disciples that went along, following the Pied Piper!

The twelve-day trip was a whirlwind tour of some magnificent gardens, too many to mention. However, I would be remiss not to mention a select few.

Sissinghurst Castle Garden is considered one of the great gardens of the world. The ten acres are divided by hedges and walls into "rooms," each with a different motif. The seasonal gardens with color schemes of white, yellow, orange, blue, and purple were stunning and unforgettable.

We toured the magnificent 180-acre Hillier Arboretum, which contains the largest collection of hardy trees and shrubs in the world. Dirr spent his sabbatical in the middle of the gardens and arboretum in 1999, and he said each morning he would roll out of bed "into heaven" with 12,000 different woody and herbaceous plants.

We stopped at the Longstock Park Water Garden, regarded as the most elegantly designed and planted water garden in all of Europe. Our trip to Stourhead, the most photographed and best-known landscaped garden in England, was a pleasure beyond belief.

We toured many other wonderful gardens, but my favorite was Powis Castle with its grand terraces preserved from the historic formal gardens of the seventeenth century. Dirr and I were strolling together on a high terrace cas-

tle walkway when we both spotted with stunning joy the Athens, Georgia–introduced homestead purple verbena (*Verbena canadensis* 'Homestead Purple'). This vigorous grower was discovered by Dr. Armitage and Dr. Dirr while driving down a back road together. They both noticed this beautiful cluster of dark purple flowers in front of an old home and slammed on the brakes, spun around, stopped, and knocked on the door. An elderly lady appeared, and at their interest in the flowers, gave them permission to take cuttings. They introduced this plant, and as Armitage said, it "kicked the verbena market in the backside!" It was thrilling to be with Dirr on this subsequent trip and see that Athens plant he co-introduced prominently displayed in Powis Castle in Wales.

Historic Hampton Court with its noble lime (*Tilia cordata*) trees, and Kew Royal Botanic Gardens, situated on the Thames, were wonderful gardens we also visited. No better way to conclude this incredible garden excursion than at Bodnant Gardens (Wales) where the magnificent rhododendrons are nestled on the steep slopes of the Conwy Valley, where the rushing water of the river Hraethlyn down the valley provides a reflective romantic sight. Bodnant was a favorite of our good friend Fred Hooks, and I recall how excited he was that day.

At most every garden we were greeted at the entrance

by large concentrations of sweet mockorange (*Philadephus coronarius*) in full bloom. The fragrance was breathtaking. We were determined to bring some home, so we researched and found the best fragrant cultivars were 'Beauclerk' and 'Belle Etoile', two hybrids I brought home to my garden. Both are doing well but have yet to reach the blooming and fragrant glory of old England.

Everybody got carried away at the various nurseries and loaded up with plants. We had a memorable "wash down" party, necessary to bring the plants back bare-rooted as required by immigration. We toasted each plant during the wash down! The party is still talked about whenever there is a reunion of some of the plant lovers that made the trip.

I brought home other plants that got my attention in addition to the sweet mockorange. Most are still doing well in the garden. I was intrigued by the brilliant yellow colors of the golden honeylocust (*Gleditsia triacanthos* f. *nermis* 'Sunburst') and brought a small one home that has grown into a nice small tree. Unfortunately it does not produce the brilliant gold color I saw in England. Could it be plants grow better on the British Isles? I did bring home two Japanese dogwoods that are doing well. Both came from the famous Spinners Nursery, Boldre. One dogwood is a weeper (*Cornus kousa*) called 'Lustgarten Weeping' and the other is *Cornus kousa* 'Satomi' with deep pink bracts. I also brought home a new Parrotia introduction, *Parrotia persica* 'Vanessa'. It has a narrower habit with brilliant autumn color and is a fast grower, now reaching about fifteen feet in the garden.

After returning from our English garden trip in 1999 I was anticipating the next studies abroad, which I assumed would be soon. As it turned out it was seven years. The reason for the long interval is because Dr. Dirr, who sets the study tone, started a love affair with a plant that was never before high on his list. For a good while hydrangeas were not among his most favorite plants until he met and

Longstock Water Garden

Powis Castle

Kew, Queen's Garden

Hampton Court, Formal Garden

Bodnant Gardens, The Dell

Philadelphus 'Belle Etoile'
Mockorange

named the remontant (reblooming) 'Endless Summer®'. This encounter embarked him on an extensive study of hydrangeas that resulted in the publication of a superb book on the subject. The newfound passion for hydrangeas finally led Dirr and his disciples to the next study abroad.

SOUTH AFRICA—THE FLORAL KINGDOM

"Don't just go, LEAD!" That was the motto of the unique "Global LEAD" University of Georgia Studies Abroad program to Cape Town, South Africa, in 2009. Barbara and I were invited to participate, and we jumped at the opportunity. We had been there before and wanted to return. Barbara thought it was one of the most beautiful places she had ever been. I wanted to return primarily to study the unique floral kingdom I had been introduced to several years before. We both got much more than we bargained for spending two weeks with fifty amazing Georgia students.

The Global LEAD program is headed by our good friends Garrett Graveson, Robbie Reese, Courtney Doran, and Kevin Scott, all of UGA HERO fame. HERO is a highly successful nonprofit program that our football coach,

Mark Richt, and I have supported for the past several years. The noble cause raises the quality of life for children affected and infected by HIV and AIDS.

LEAD is an acronym for Leadership, Education, Adventure, and Diplomacy (service), which represent the four pillars of the program. What separates it from other studies abroad programs is the diplomacy or service component, which as cofounder Kevin Scott said, enables students not only to "train their minds but also to train from their heart."

As an example, all fifty students, broken into ten teams of five, went to a township and completely restored an abandoned classroom. When they finished, the teacher and many of the students were in tears of celebration, especially as the children demonstrated their playful excitement. Similar services were performed throughout the six-week LEAD course.

In addition to lecturing on leadership and teamwork, my task was to lead the students on a tour of the world-famous Kirstenbosch Garden and to give a brief overview of the unique floral kingdom of South Africa. This world-famous botanical garden is located on the lower eastern slopes of Cape Town's Table Mountain, and the view of the mountain rising almost straight up is spectacular. That assignment led me to a fascinating study of the Cape floral kingdom.

Here are a few facts that grabbed my attention and convinced me why the South Africa floral kingdom is regarded in a league of its own.

It is the smallest and richest of the world's six floral kingdoms and the only one contained in one country. It represents only 0.04 percent of the Earth's land. Contrast that with the fact that the largest floral kingdom (Boreal), which we are a part of in the United States, represents almost 42 percent, covering an area from the Arctic about halfway down the entire globe. The other four regions consist basically of Central and South America, the rest of Africa, Australia, and the bottom tip of South America.

There are 9,600-plus plant species crammed into the Cape floral kingdom and about 6,200 are endemic, found nowhere else on Earth. On the spectacular and breathtaking Table Mountain in Cape Town alone there are over 2,200 species—more than in the entire United Kingdom!

The dominant flora of the Cape floral region is Fynbos, meaning "fine brush" in Afrikaans. I was surprised to learn it grows on coarse-grained, low-nutrient, acidic sand soil. The "fine brush" refers to the fine needlelike leaves of many Fynbos species, the majority of which can be broken down into three plant families—*Protea* (Proteaceae), the Cape Heaths (Heath) or *Erica* (Ericaceae), and the Restios (Restionaceae) or grasslike reeds.

Erica (heather) is a large genus with well over 600 species, all but about 26 belonging to South Africa. Because of the wide range of species, there are different types of flowers throughout the year. The long-tubed species attracts brilliantly colored sunbirds with their long beaks, which pollinate them as they probe the flower for nectar. The red and yellow *Erica* 'Prince of Wales' was the popular bird choice when we visited that year in May.

My encounter with the plant heather (*Calluna*), the low, hardy variety, was on a national coaches' Scotland golf trip many years ago. I spent most of my playing time trying to get my golf balls out of the heather! I gave up golf after that trip, never to play again thanks to the heather and a Scottish caddy who told me after a round that I was "a nice lad but I need some golf lessons!" Gardening became my golf from that point on.

There are about 300 cape reeds species, and they occur in all the different habitats, contrasted to *Erica* and *Protea*, and are thus the defining plants of the Fynbos. However, their tiny flowers are unspectacular. Their appeal lies in their form, texture, and foliage color, but they pale in comparison to the family Proteaceae.

If I had my wish of two plants that I could grow in my garden (but impossible) it would be the Sino-Himalayan *Magnolia campbellii* that I saw in the southwest (Cornwall) part of England and the family Proteaceae, primarily the genera *Protea*, *Leucadendron*, and *Leucospermum* of South Africa.

I would give the *Protea* (sugar bush) the most valuable genus award if I were a plant judge. While they grow in Australia and New Zealand, there are over a hundred species that grow in South Africa alone. The national flower is the king protea (*Protea cynaroides*). The beautiful flower consists of large brightly colored bracts that surround a compact-type flower in a color variety of red, pink, yellow, white, and green. The king protea has flower heads up to six inches with widely spaced bracts that vary in colors of white, silver, pink, rose pink, or crimson. With their strong stems they are magnificent cut flowers. Barbara fell in love with them and is determined to have them dried and used as a mainstay throughout the house. In the family with the *Protea* are *Leucadendron* and *Leucospermum*, which are also spectacular.

Leucadendron (cone bush) comprises a genus of seventy evergreen species in South Africa. The distinctive flowers (male and female) on different plants are surrounded by bractlike leaves that color up handsomely during spring and winter in practically every possible color. One of the most interesting species is the twenty-foot silver tree (*Leucadendron argenteum*), which is an awesome sight in mass alongside Signal Mountain overlooking the city where a cannon has been fired daily for over two centuries at high noon.

Just as spectacular is *Leucospermum* 'Pincushion' flower. There are about fifty species in the family Proteaceae, and the flower provides dense inflorescences with a large number of prominent styles that prompted the name 'Pincushion' flower. Like the *Protea*, the *Leucadendron* and *Leucospermum* are also marvelous, highly decorative, with long-lasting cut flowers.

One of the most interesting protea species is *Protea florida* called 'Blushing Bride', the same cultivar name Dirr gave to one of his hydrangea crosses that produces a white mophead that turns pink like the blush of a bride. The small white-that-turns-pink *Protea* 'Blushing Bride' flower is worn on the lapel of suitors who are proposing marriage to a young damsel. Tradition says that if the flower has already turned pink, it behooves the damsel to say no, since that means the flower is "fading out" like the suitor.

This research had me well prepared to walk the Kirstenbosch Garden and expound my knowledge to those who wanted to listen. It wasn't necessary to impart my knowledge too much, since the students were awestruck with the magnificent scenery of the gardens and wandered off in small groups.

Several of the students fulfilled the stringent requirements given by Georgia's horticulture professor Cecelia McGregor, who is originally from South Africa. To qualify for the three-hour credit the students were required to write two ten-page, single-spaced papers describing the unique floral kingdom and how plants are used in everyday life in South Africa. In addition they were required to choose ten plants from Kirstenbosch Botanical Gardens and ten from Table Mountain, describing their botanical name, usage, and origin. They also had to choose from a long list of fifteen plants to describe in detail. The requirement also called for two pages of pictures. Finally the students chose ten base plants for food, describing how they are cooked and used, such as for tea, etc. Tough requirements? Yes, for most, but not for these gifted students.

I went back to the garden on another occasion and quietly strolled through the areas beyond the Fynbos vegetation. Though not in its spring glory, there were isolated blooms of the orange bird of paradise (*Strelitzia*), a symbol of the garden. In honor of President Nelson Mandela, the world hero of South Africa, there is a gold form of the bird of paradise called 'Mandela's Gold' that took twenty years to hybridize, which amazed the students. Another most interesting plant was the scented leaf *Pelagonium scabrum* that is known as the father of all geranium plants. The list of unique plants I stumbled upon could go on and on, but I would be remiss if I didn't mention two trees that brought me back to my garden in Athens.

The first was a *Ginkgo biloba* (Maiden hair tree), whose leaves were just turning yellow during our May (autumn in South Africa) visit. I have two of those ancient living fossils in my garden. The ginkgo has a fascinating history. It is one of the oldest trees growing and can be traced back over 150 million years ago. I have an upright fast-growing form and an interesting dwarf form called 'Witches Broom'. I also stumbled upon an incredible blue Atlas cedar (*Cedrus atlantica* 'Glauca'). This was the bluest blue Atlas (Atlas Mountains of northwest Africa) cedar I have ever seen. I

Protea cynaroides
King Protea

The unique yet fragile Cape floral region area was declared a World Heritage Site by the United Nations in 2004 under its program UNESCO. That same year Kirstenbosch National Botanical Garden became the first garden in the world to receive this honor.

As a matter of interest UNESCO (United Nations Economic Scientific and Cultural Organizations) was organized to preserve and protect world cultural and natural sites. It started in 1959 when UNESCO saved the Abu Simbel Temple in Egypt after flooding by the Aswan Dam. Thanks to international pressure, the temple was moved to a new location. Barbara and I and hundreds of thousands more have enjoyed this Egyptian treasure in its new location, and millions more will enjoy it in the future, thanks to UNESCO.

Because the Cape floral region was declared a world protective area, the Cape is managed by South African National Biodiversity Institute and National Parks. The declaration has also aroused awareness among its citizens. This was evident when the Global LEAD group visited Haut Espoir (High Hope) Vineyard in the Franschoek Valley. This beautiful valley was granted to the French Huguenots in the seventeenth century and they soon used their wine skills to start the highly successful South African wine industry. The Haut Espoir Winery is a member of the Biodiversity and Wine Institute, whose mission is to minimize further losses of the natural habitat of the Cape floral kingdom and contribute to sustainable wine production practices. The Haut Espoir Winery has removed alien vegetation, such as pines and blue gums (both notorious earth water suckers), and dedicated three hectares (7.41316 acres) of mountain land to reestablishing natural Fynbos floral species that now surround the area. The winery even has a nursery that is set up to grow *Protea, Erica,* and other species of the area. The South

stood mesmerized for a while looking at that wide-spreading, bright Kentucky blue specimen. The blue Atlas cedar is very trainable, and I have two beautiful architectural forms in my garden. Both were given to me by my friend and highly regarded Atlanta landscape architect Ed Castro, who personally placed the trees in the garden. He had one of his top assistants, Fred Barber Jr., actually plant the tree. Ironically Fred Jr. is the son of Fred Barber Sr., one of my first left halfbacks and hero of the Sun Bowl in 1964, now a pharmacist in Blackshear, Georgia.

In my garden the first blue (not so blue compared to the South African blue) Atlas cedar is shaped like a cascading arch and serves as the entrance to a path by the pond and sunroom. The second one is eight feet tall and shaped like an upright swirling boa constrictor (a popular Japanese-trained leader) located in the entrance of the dwarf conifer garden near the street.

Protea cynaroides
King Protea

Leucospermum cirtitum
Pin Cushion Flower

Africans are aware of their evolutionary treasure thanks to UNESCO and its declaration of the area as a World Heritage Site. Had it been long neglected or lost, it would have been gone forever.

The South African floral pride got another boost when the Royal Horticultural Society's Chelsea Flower Show in London, billed as the world's International Floral Olympics, awarded two gold medals in May 2009. One gold medal went to the experienced Kirstenbosch team whose design was entitled "Haven of Biodiversity." This

was the thirtieth win by the garden in the thirty-four years of competition. The real excitement came when the city of Durbin, only in its third year of competing, won South Africa's second gold.

The entire South African floral experience was exciting and rewarding. My appreciation goes to the young turks of Global LEAD who allowed me to see firsthand that our country under these future generation of leaders is in good hands and to experience firsthand a personal studies abroad program of a floral kingdom.

CHAPTER FIVE

FALLING
FOR HYDRANGEAS

THE INTERNATIONAL HYDRANGEA CONFERENCE

The historic city of Ghent, Belgium, the biggest city in the world next to Paris in the Middle Ages, was the site of the International Hydrangea Conference in August 2007. The energetic but calm Luc Balemans of the Belgium Hydrangea Society did a remarkable job putting together the conference of 160 hydrangea enthusiasts from fifteen countries. The conference was held at the Ghent University Botanical Garden. World-renowned hydrangea plantsmen conducted dozens of seminars, and we toured four spectacular gardens. I found myself in the middle of all of this wondering once again, "What in the world am I doing here?" The answer (by the grace of Dirr) was similar to some of my other horticulture predicaments. I'd run into Dirr and a few of his buddies at the Southern Nursery meeting in Atlanta in early August 2007, and he'd suggested, "Why don't you go to Belgium with us for the International Hydrangea Society meeting?" Thinking he was referring to next summer I said, "When?" He answered, "Next Tuesday." I replied, "*Next* Tuesday?" and laughed it off, thinking it wasn't possible. Nevertheless I mentioned it to Barbara, and overnight on her computer she made flight and hotel reservations compatible with Dirr's schedule. I was amazed.

When I was coaching, Barbara always complained I traveled too much, and now she works miracles for me to leave! Dirr got me registered for the sold-out conference, and I was soon on my way to join Dirr and his group the next day in the Brussels airport. After renting a car and driving to Ghent, we joined the conference of some of the greatest hydrangea experts and enthusiasts in the world.

Heading the list from the United States was our own Dr. Michael Dirr, whose recent book on hydrangeas had the conference buzzing. Using as a topic "New Hydrangeas for American Gardens," Dirr explored some of the advances in breeding and marketing that have set the hydrangea market on fire in the United States.

He pointed to Martha Stewart's advocacy, the founding of the American Hydrangea Society by the late Penny McHenry of Atlanta, and books by himself, Toni Lawson-Hall, and Cor and Dick Van Gelderen as playing a part in reinvigorating the interest in hydrangea. What really stimulated the general public was the introduction of a remontant (reblooming) cultivar of *Hydrangea macrophylla* appropriately named by Dirr 'Endless Summer®'. The plant was discovered in a St. Paul, Minnesota, garden by a Bailey's Nursery employee, Vern Black. Dirr saw the plant in September in flower and was flabbergasted. He later determined this was the first *Hydrangea macrophylla*, a species that historically blooms on the old wood, to bloom on both the old and new wood! The added fact that the plant was cold-hardy to zone 4 made this a startling discovery. This remarkable plant, however, was no different in one respect than other hydrangeas of this species. Acidic soil produced blue flowers and alkaline soil produced pink flowers.

After further testing of the plant by Bailey's Nursery the plant was released in 2004, and within five years over seven million had been sold.

Meanwhile with the Endless Summer® super success,

Hydrangea macrophylla Endless Summer™ collection
Endless Summer®, Twist-n-Shout™, and 'Blushing Bride'
Bigleaf Hydrangea

Dr. Dirr started a new business endeavor called Plant Introductions, Inc., which he partnered with his good friends Mark Griffith and Jeff Beasley, two Dirr disciples and highly respected nurserymen. The other member of the team is Josh Kardos, a new Ph.D. graduate who is the resident plant-breeding expert. Since I know them all well and most live in Athens, except Beasley who lives in nearby Lavonia, I am up-to-date on what is happening in their wonderful breeding world, especially hydrangeas.

As Dirr told the international conference, "The remontants (rebloomers) are the future!" This phenomenon follows the reblooming (Encore®) azaleas that have taken the market by storm. Dirr pointed out to the conference that his hydrangea improvement program has developed 'Blushing Bride', an Endless Summer® cross with 'Veitchii'. I have several in my garden, and they open pure white and turn blush pink (sometimes blush blue) on the edges. Also 'Mini Penny', a dwarf reblooming seedling of 'Penny Mac', was introduced by UGA (University of Georgia). UGA plant, Twist-n-Shout™, a reblooming pink lacecap that I followed before it was named, was introduced by Plant Introductions, Inc.

'Penny Mac' times 'Lady in Red' produced this pink lacecap that is a blooming machine, an apt description; I have several that are constant bloomers. Dirr was particularly excited, and I was with him when he introduced the new cross to some horticulture enthusiasts. At the time he was looking for an appropriate name. One lady suggested that since it was crossed with 'Lady in Red' and is a consistent rebloomer, call it 'Always a Lady'; both Dirr and I thought it was the perfect name with a classy touch, and the women who heard the name swooned. Not so with the expert marketing team of Bailey's Nursery, who gave it the name Twist-n-Shout™, a name I am still trying to get used to. If spending money is any indication of Bailey's marketing ability, Twist-n-Shout™ will be a huge success. I was a firsthand observer of their 2009 hydrangea promotion.

Dr. Dirr asked me if Bailey's could come by my garden and take a few pictures, to which I readily agreed. They obviously liked my garden setting so I was flattered. Little did I, or Dirr, know that "a few pictures" were a full-blown, three-full-day production shoot. This shoot turned out to be the biggest and most elaborate I have ever seen—and I have seen and been involved in some big photo productions in my forty-plus years as a coach and athletic director.

They had abundant technical equipment and artistic skill as they staged various scenes throughout the garden. They used the new introduction Twist-n-Shout™ along with the other proven remontant winners Endless Summer® and 'Blushing Bride'. Barbara and I watched in amazement as they artistically set up these gorgeous scenes and then waited on the porch of our pool house for the sun to be just right before taking the pictures. The shoot was part of a public relations campaign designed to reach "over 150 million customers of Bailey's." In several publications, including *Southern Living*, I saw full-page ads of

Hydrangea macrophylla Twist-n-Shout™
Bigleaf Hydrangea

the Endless Summer® collection with our garden as the backdrop. Our white Japanese bridges that span the creek were particularly noticeable in the ads.

As a way of thanks, I was pleased that the crew left me with several of the Endless Summer® and 'Blushing Bride' plants as well as a couple of Twist-n-Shout™ when they finished. I was hoping for a few more of the Twist-n-Shout™, but they were obviously in short supply of the new introduction at the time. Nevertheless I have a couple of nice beds of these young remontant winners that put on quite a display in mass. Dirr later supplied me with several more, which are planted next to the creek, shaded by a special anniversary Japanese maple. Others are planted under a southern magnolia (*Magnolia grandiflora*) near the rustic bridge that crosses the creek.

Dirr told the international conference there were two other hydrangea projects in the making that I was proudly aware of, since many times my garden has become one of the testing grounds. For example, I have a number of plants, many hydrangeas in particular that are not named but carry a testing designation such as V-01-09 or DR-02-06. The former letter (V) refers to hydrangea 'Veitchii', which is a good parent for breeding, and the latter (DR) to

Hydrangea arborescens Bella Anna™
Smooth Hydrangea

'David Ramsey', a proven remontant bloomer. I have numerous plants listed by letters and numbers that will never be officially named but most are worthy selections that simply did not get the nod. On occasions Dirr has walked our garden and done a double-take on what he thought was a number-two or number-three plant that he thinks now should have been a number one. I enjoy telling him he is always welcome to take cuttings of my plants.

Dirr and his plant introduction team are constantly looking for plant improvement that includes hardiness, disease resistance, heat tolerance, compact habit, strong stems, dark green leaves, superior flowers, and of course remontant characteristics.

I do have a selection of *Dichroa febrifuga* (an evergreen hydrangea relative), which was crossed with *Hydrangea macrophylla* and will eventually be "backcrossed" in an effort to create an evergreen hydrangea with blue berries and fixed blue blossoms.

Meanwhile I have patiently waited for over a year to receive an exciting hydrangea that Dr. Dirr and his team had been working on for almost ten years—a pink 'Annabelle' (*Hydrangea arborescens*). I went out to the plant-introduction nursery where Dirr pointed it out to me

in bloom, and it looked fantastic!

Meanwhile this new plant had been given the impressive name Bella Anna™ a reversal of 'Annabelle'. I returned to the nursery shortly thereafter and Dr. Dirr, unable to restrain himself, gave me a prize Bella Anna™ in full bloom. I immediately put it in a pot in the patio. The timing was perfect! A few days later we put on a fund-raiser for the Southeastern Horticulture Society that drew over a hundred plant enthusiasts. The star of the show was the pink Bella Anna™. I never heard so many "wows" in one gathering. The white 'Annabelle' has been a real winner in the marketplace and the pink Bella Anna™ ought to cause the market to do a flip.

DON SHADOW FILL-IN

Don Shadow of Winchester, Tennessee, one of the most respected plantsmen in the industry, was scheduled to speak in Ghent at the hydrangea conference, but an illness prevented him. Sandra Reed of the United States National Arboretum in Tennessee spoke on his behalf. Reed told the international group that *Hydrangea arborescens* (smooth hydrangea) and *Hydrangea quercifolia* (oakleaf hydrangea) were the only two hydrangeas native to the United States. Most of the cultivars of these two species were selected from the wild or as chance seedlings in nurseries and gardens. The most recent kind with commercial potential is the *Hydrangea arborescens* 'Hayes Starburst' with "double florets held away from the main inflorescence on long pedicels, thereby giving a starburst effect." Reed also mentioned a fragrant *Hydrangea arborescens* yet unnamed and a pink-flowered *Hydrangea arborescens* called 'Wesser Falls' with fertile flowers, which Dirr and his breeding partner Dr. Kardos used, along with 'Eco Pink Puff', to produce the pink Bella Anna™.

Reed made reference to my home state of Alabama, where most of the double inflorescence *Hydrangea quercifolia* (oakleaf hydrangea) have been found. 'Snowflake', cultivated and promoted by Eddie Aldridge of Birmingham some forty years ago, set the standard for the double-flowering oakleaf. Aldridge also introduced 'Harmony', a thick double-flowered rounded plant with a compact habit.

Reed claims that new discoveries in Alabama of double inflorescences (actually sterile flowers with sepals that cover the fertile flowers) may be superior to the industry standards discovered by Aldridge. For instance, she said 'Brother Edward' and 'Emerald Lake' are both more rounded than 'Harmony', and 'Suma Tanga Star' may be superior to 'Snowflake'. That statement aroused my curiosity since my friend Eddie Aldridge gave me both 'Snowflake' and 'Harmony', and they are marvelous additions to the garden. During the rest of Reed's lecture, I started thinking about going to my home state to see firsthand what she was talking about.

Reed got my attention again toward the end of her lecture. She pointed out the initiation of a new breeding program to develop compact *Hydrangea quercifolia* in Tennessee. The study also included taking 1,500 oakleaf seedlings from controlled pollinations of 'Snow Queen' and 'Pee Wee' for evaluating and testing to find some that might be released as cultivars. In 2010 Dr. Reed introduced 'Munchkin' and 'Ruby Slippers' that resulted from the oakleaf breeding. That was interesting, but I kept thinking about those new finds in Alabama. Since my attention was focused on my home state, I will temporarily leave the conference and fast-forward to my Alabama hydrangea journey and my friend Eddie Aldridge, a gentleman and plantsman of the first order.

EDDIE ALDRIDGE

A discussion of hydrangeas would not be complete without a reference to my friend Eddie Aldridge who patented

Hydrangea quercifolia 'Snowflake'
Oakleaf Hydrangea

the famous oakleaf hydrangea 'Snowflake' (*Hydrangea quercifolia* 'Snowflake'). I believe it is the most beautiful of all the sterile-flowered forms as well as all the many oakleaf cultivars. What separates 'Snowflake' from most of the rest of the species is while hydrangea flowers usually produce four sepals, 'Snowflake' forms multiple sepals on the floret with no seeds, thereby producing multiple double flowers over the entire panicle. The spectacular panicles are over a foot long, and the beauty lasts for about eight weeks, which includes the gradual color change to maroon of the stacked sepals at the bottom of the florets.

Eddie related the fascinating history of the plant to me. A neighbor from Lipscomb, Alabama, just south of Birmingham, brought a bloom to Eddie's father for identification in June 1969. The plant had been resting next to Turkey Creek in that town since 1923. Eddie's father, Loren L. Aldridge, who played football at Auburn and graduated in 1927, was a highly respected nurseryman. Ironically, he ran a retail store not far from where Barbara grew up in Homewood, Alabama, and her parents were frequent customers. Barbara remembers going into the nursery many times, meeting Eddie, his father, and especially his mother, who Barbara said "was always there."

When Aldridge first saw the flower, he knew it would be a winner, but nothing was ever done until Eddie got the plant patented, as he said, for "publicity purposes more than anything else." Even then it was seven years before the plant got on the market, despite a calamity that could have resulted in a disastrous end to 'Snowflake'.

The original plant died, but Eddie was able to get three cuttings and had them potted up and eventually put in the ground, and all three were doing well. However, one day in an obvious miscommunication, a garden laborer assigned to pulling weeds pulled the hydrangeas and threw the three plants in a Dumpster, and Eddie "threw the laborer in headfirst after them!" They were able to retrieve the plants, but two died, leaving only one cutting that survived to become the source of all the 'Snowflake' plants in existence.

I am sure that without 'Snowflake' there would not have been the Aldridge botanical garden that has been such a blessing to Birmingham and the city of Hoover. Eddie and his lovely wife Kay have poured their heart, soul, and finances into this garden, which in addition to having an extensive display of hydrangeas and native plants provides a wonderful playground and learning experience for children. They call it a "Garden of Destiny." A book they wrote and financed by the same name describes how the garden, dedicated to the memory of Eddie's late father, mother, and brother, was "just meant to be."

Eddie gave me a personal tour of the garden in the summer of 2009 when all the 'Snowflake' hydrangeas were in bloom. It seemed there were hundreds of them, all ten feet tall with their magnificent cascading inflorescences. Many of the 'Snowflake' were stock plants when Eddie was living and working there before the conversion to the botanical garden. Eddie also pointed out the "Georgia collection" in the garden, which he said should have been called the "Dirr Collection," since Dirr generously gave to the garden 164 varieties of hydrangeas.

Eddie also pointed to 'Harmony', the sterile oakleaf hydrangea he propagated and introduced. 'Harmony' can grow up to ten feet, displaying large, thick twelve-inch-long and eight-inch-wide inflorescences. The plant was discovered in the wild in the 1920s and transplanted to Rainbow City, near Gadsden, Alabama, in the Harmony Baptist Church cemetery by the father of the late J. C. McDaniel, formerly of Alabama. Ironically, McDaniel, a plantsman extraordinaire, was the eccentric horticulture professor at the University of Illinois who Dirr said "schooled" him when they were professors there together. The McDaniels and the Aldridges were longtime friends, which accounts for the fact Eddie was allowed to propagate the plant. When I was in Birmingham several years ago to speak to the Birmingham Botanical Garden as part of a lecture series to honor the lovely Mrs. Virginia Spence, a gracious lady and the mother of one of my former players, Hal Bissell, Eddie gave me two five-gallon containers of 'Snowflake' and 'Harmony', and they have been mainstays in the garden.

There are four other completely sterile flowers like 'Harmony' that Eddie describes as one-in-a-million-chance seedlings. One was found and patented by my friend Vaughn Billingsley in Rabun County, Georgia, called 'Vaughn's Lillie', after Billingsley's wife who, interestingly, is the sister of James and Walt Stancil, who built our house on Lake Burton. Dirr and I saw the plant in the Billingsley's valley garden just north of Clayton, and he knew it was something special. Dirr guided Billingsley in his patent pursuit. I have two 'Vaughn's Lillie', one in my garden at home and one at the lake house. It is a beautiful flower but unfortunately the deer think it is one of the most delicious meals in my garden. Because of its deer appeal, I apply a little Deer Off to it and a few other deer delicacies from time to time. Since the north Georgia mountain deer have different taste buds or the plant is in a "no deer zone," 'Vaughn Lillie' puts on quite a show while all the family is there for the annual July 4 reunion celebration.

There are a few other similar sterile-flowered oakleaf hydrangeas such as 'Wade Mahlke', which also carries the name 'Emerald Lake', since it was found by Wade Mahlke beside the lake near Pinson, Alabama, in Jefferson County. It is similar but has bigger flowers than the others, and the humble gentleman told me he prefers the name be 'Emerald Lake', because it "sounds better than just old Wade Mahlke."

The other sterile oakleaf inflorescence is 'Roanoke', the only one I have not seen in person. Dirr describes the flower as "loose and more open" than 'Harmony'. He said there is a "massive planting at Bernheim arboretum" in Kentucky that is "ten feet high and thirty feet wide" that he saw in 1997. It is interesting that I have not been able to find a history of the origin of the plant. Eddie Aldridge shared a letter with me that led to an investigation, the results of which are as follows. Professor McDaniel was traveling through his home state of Alabama after attending a horticulture conference in New Orleans. He spotted this sterile hydrangea at a home in Roanoke, Alabama, and asked the lady of the house for cuttings. The lady was turned off by what she believed to be an "eccentric Yankee" and told him, "No!"

Not to be denied, McDaniel, the persistent southerner who attended Auburn, came back later at night and took cuttings in a dramatic watermelon-type caper known as the "midnight cuttings" affair. He took the cuttings home to the University of Illinois at Urbana-Champaign and grew them in the greenhouse. He later introduced and named the plant 'Roanoke', but for obvious reasons never revealed the history of the find.

The remarkable Sara Duke Groves, a close horticulture friend of the late professor McDaniel, rode with him from the New Orleans horticulture conference. She later shared a letter from McDaniel about the incident with her good friend Doug Reynolds. I have gotten to know Doug (a fellow infected horticulturist) through Eddie Aldridge. Reynolds introduced me to Sara, and I had a wonderful visit with the fascinating woman. The letter McDaniel wrote to Sara in 1968, among other things, gave a "cutting" update of their trip. McDaniel wrote that "the loot I got back to Urbana is growing in the greenhouse" and "the hydrangea (midnight) cuttings from Roanoke are breaking bud." The letter puts to rest, like Professor McDaniel, the unknown history of 'Roanoke'.

The last of the big-five compact sterile-flowered oakleaf flowers is 'Brother Edwards', a cultivar found by Doug and Brenda Hill, who run Blackwood Crossing Nursery in Cleveland, Alabama. They named the plant after their Baptist minister there in Blount County. The 'Brother Edwards' is smaller and more compact and rounded than the other sterile cultivars and fades to a beautiful light green. I visited the Hills at their nursery and saw firsthand 'Brother Edwards' and a few other unique finds.

These big-five unique sterile cultivars are all beautiful, but the one downside is the flowers are entirely too heavy for the branches, even more so after they get wet. An ideal situation for those heavy inflorescences would be to rest them on the strong stems of a new oakleaf seedling produced by Hill from "thousands of seedlings" from the oakleaf cultivar 'Snow Queen', a successful upright cultivar. Hill calls the selection 'Snow Princess', and the flowers are impressive in their upright form even more so than their 'Snow Queen' mother.

During my visit to Hill's nursery, he introduced me to another interesting hydrangea find, a fragrant *H. arborescens* (smooth hydrangea). Hill named it 'Mary Faye' after the wife of 'Brother Edwards'. The most familiar *H. arborescens* is 'Annabelle', one of the most beloved plants in America. Dirr describes the sterile white mophead as "the queen of the arborescens." The two 'Annabelle' in my garden by the pool

Hydrangea arborescens 'Annabelle'
Smooth Hydrangea

area have been spectacular performers that last all summer with their white-to-green mophead display. Of course, as mentioned previously, there is now pink Bella Anna™, destined to be one of the next great plants.

Hill's *H. arborescens* is a lacecap with an extremely pleasant fragrance. I will be interested to watch to see if 'Mary Faye' is received by the market. For sure the public will like the fragrance.

By far the most exciting thing in the Hills' Blackwood Nursery is a new oakleaf that has all the characteristics of the world-famous 'Snowflake'. I first heard about this new plant at the International Hydrangea Conference, and later, while riding in the backseat of Don Shadow's truck touring his nursery with Dirr, I was all ears when I heard Shadow tell Dirr about an Indian-named oakleaf 'Suma Tanga Star'. My curiosity got the best of me, and the second hearing was the charm that finally set me off on the Alabama hydrangea journey.

I contacted Eddie Aldridge about 'Suma Tanga Star' because I heard in the discussion that it resembles 'Snowflake'. Eddie knew the entire history and more. He told me his aunt Clustie McIntyre, a forty-year biology teacher from Hueytown, Alabama, whom he describes as

Hydrangea paniculata 'Phantom'
Panicle Hydrangea

Hydrangea quercifolia, fall color
Oakleaf Hydrangea

"the first environmentalist," was the first to find the plant at the Methodist camp Suma Tanga Chapel in St. Claire County, Alabama. Eddie and his father visited the site and earlier thought it was the same as 'Snowflake'; however after visiting the plant again and later with Don Shadow, he concluded the plant was different from 'Snowflake' and contacted his friend Doug Hill in nearby Cleveland, encouraging him to propagate the plant.

After consultation with Aldridge, Shadow, and Hill and observing the plant firsthand, I noticed a definite difference from 'Snowflake', particularly in the flower. While both inflorescences have sepals stacked on top of each other, forming the double-flowering effect, the 'Suma Tanga Star' sepals are more pointed and compact than 'Snowflake'. Eddie, who took three cuttings a few years ago, describes the plant as a little more dwarf than 'Snowflake' and told me that the renowned plantsman from New Zealand, Glyn Church, said that the "constitution of 'Suma Tanga Star' is not quite as strong as 'Snowflake'."

Because of the pointed sepals of the flower, Eddie thinks that the best name for the plant is 'Starlight' because it describes perfectly the floral appearance. He also believes the Indian name is too complicated and has relayed his feelings to his friend Doug Hill. Aldridge is held in high esteem by Hill, and he is weighing heavily Eddie's 'Starlight' preference. Hill, who has taken hundreds of cuttings from the original plant, is negotiating with Spring Meadow Nursery, who could be involved in naming rights and marketing. It will be interesting to watch the rest of the story. Meanwhile Doug and Brenda have given me a trial-basis small sample of 'Suma Tanga Star' ('Starlight'), the oakleaf 'Brother Edwards', the fragrant *H. arborescens* 'Mary Faye', and the upright oakleaf 'Snow Princess'. They shared their treasures knowing I am just an interested plantsman and not a competitive nurseryman.

Eddie, who has been retired for several years and is no longer a competitive nurseryman, is enjoying life in his new home in a beautiful mountain-lake subdivision south of Birmingham. I stayed in his home on my hydrangea journey in the summer of 2009. His lovely wife, Kay, was a marvelous hostess while Eddie and I toured the garden around the house. Eddie spends time each morning working the garden and pausing to admire those ten-feet 'Snowflake' with the beautiful flowers cascading down toward the lake. Before he took me on the Aldridge garden tour, we stopped by Hannah's Nursery to acquire Eddie's latest find. The trip to the nursery stirred some vivid memories of an earlier visit when I first became "infected."

Eddie had earlier told me about his most recent find in the wild, a fragrant 'PeeGee' hydrangea (*H. paniculata* 'Grandiflora'). Like other good nurserymen, his eyes are always trained to look for something new wherever his travels take him. He was driving about six miles out of Brevard, North Carolina, on Highway 64 while Kay was sleeping when he spotted this 'PeeGee' hydrangea with the biggest blooms he'd ever seen. He slammed on the brakes, apologized for waking her up, and turned the car around to find this mass of fragrant 'PeeGee' hydrangea, whose sepals he described as "so close together they have to be lifted to enjoy the fragrance." He encouraged his friends at Hannah Nursery to propagate them under the name of 'Mountain Fragrant', since the original plant was found at an elevation of 2,400 feet. I picked up a plant and related my experience with Hannah Nursery to the young manager David Shaddix.

I told David that the first oakleaf I planted in my garden after I got the bug came from this nursery when Steve Hannah started out in the business, and the store was one-third the size. Steve is originally from Athens and the son of the late Mark Hannah, who was a business investment professor and bridge friend at Auburn. Both he and his wife, Ellen, and Barbara and I came to Georgia from Auburn about the same time. Steve, one of five sons, moved to Birmingham to start the nursery, and I was among his earliest customers. I bought two different plants from Steve that I vividly recall, since both have performed well and not overgrown their original characteristic—like all my early plantings. The first is the oakleaf hydrangea cultivar 'Pee Wee' I planted next to the street. After twelve years it is not exactly "pee wee" but has reached a six-foot apparent maximum height. The flowers have remained small, about five inches, or half the size of

Hydrangea quercifolia
Oakleaf Hydrangea

most oakleaf inflorescences. At the same time I bought a five-gallon, two-foot-high paperbark maple (*Acer griseum*). It has been in the same spot by the dry creek for twelve years and slowly grown to ten feet. It is a real favorite, and I pause to admire the dark red, exfoliating, paper bark every time I pass. Steve Hannah has many other irons in the fire and has moved to Pensacola. Eddie, who comes by often, thinks Shaddix does a superb job of managing the store for Steve. Shaddix and his lovely fiancée, Mary Beth, a Georgia graduate and horticulture enthusiast, have visited my garden.

Reflecting back on my journey to Alabama on the hydrangea chase, I was amazed at the number of oakleaf selections that came from my native state. 'Pee Wee' and many of the *H. quercifolia* cultivars came from Alabama. Four out of the top five of the sterile-flowered plants—'Harmony', 'Brother Edwards', 'Roanoke', and 'Emerald Lake'—came from Alabama. The two sterile double-flowering plants 'Snowflake' and now 'Suma Tanga Star' ('Starlight') came from Alabama. Plantsmen from the state point out, with great pride, that John Bartram, in his many travels, found and named the oakleaf hydrangea in Alabama. I tell them my research points to Georgia as the place Bartram made his discovery. They retaliate by saying when Bartram traveled in 1791, Alabama was part of the Georgia territory granted by the king of England. So I continued to search and found that Francis Harper's book on the travels of William Bartram concludes that Bartram's *Hydrangea quercifolia* find in 1776 was in present-day Henry County, Georgia, on Culpepper Creek some eight miles from the Flint River. Despite such evidence, the Alabama purists are not conceding.

One of my many enjoyments during horticultural travels is to listen to passionate plantspeople talk about their new finds. They take great pride in the special rewards that come with introducing new plants to the industry. Meanwhile I find myself while walking or driving making quick stops to investigate what might be a new find! I suppose that goes with the spreading enjoyment of my horticulture infection.

Meanwhile, now that the Alabama hydrangea journey has been satisfied, it's appropriate to go back in time to the international hydrangea conference.

THE INTERNATIONAL HYDRANGEA CONFERENCE, PART 2

After the lectures by Dr. Dirr and Sandra Reed of Tennessee, there were several other lectures on the exploration and growing of the genus around the world. Of particular interest was the origin of hydrangeas that can be traced back to China and Japan. The Japanese had the best opportunity to cultivate the species, but they never embraced the bigleaf hydrangea because of its large size and "fickle" personality of changing colors. Big and fickle are not desirable traits sought by the Japanese.

The English made an attempt to extract the hydrangeas from Japan and China and bring them to the European market. The famous Veitch Nursery sent Charles

Hydrangea macrophylla
Bigleaf Hydrangea

Maries to the Far East, and in 1879 he brought back one in particular, *Hydrangea macrophylla* 'Mariesii', a lacecap that is still available today. Two years later Maries brought back another lacecap, 'Veitchii' (after the nursery), and it too is still around today. Unfortunately, neither hydrangeas nor Maries were appreciated back in England, which was a blessing for the French. They became leaders in collecting and hybridizing the species that later became known as the French hydrangea.

The other hydrangea species grown in Japan is *H. serrata* 'Tea of Heaven', which is smaller and more readily embraced by the Japanese. The *H. serrata* species is a lifetime study. There are many good cultivars, mostly lacecaps. I have several in the garden, but my two favorites are 'Miyama Yae-murasaki', a double (part sterile) pink-to-purple lacecap, and 'Preziosa' (a hybrid of *H. serrata* × *H. macrophylla*), a true pink-red mophead. Dirr has a 'Preziosa' seedling that might turn out to be superior to the mother plant. He shared one with me, so I will be watching it with special interest.

Other lectures included Rudolf Dirr, who might have been a lost German cousin of our Dr. Dirr. He explored the European market for hydrangeas. There were technical

lectures on breeding, genes, disease, bluing, and fertilizing, all too high-tech for me, though I sat through them all. I really enjoyed the lectures by Mal Condon from Hydrangea Farm Nursery on Nantucket Island off the coast of New England, and Glyn Church, of Woodleigh Gardens in New Plymouth, New Zealand.

Condon says his farm is clearly a collector's nursery with over 200 varieties of hydrangeas. He said he is always on "the hunt for new and unusual plants from all the hydrangea growing regions of the world." Condon loves the climate in Nantucket, ideal for growing hydrangeas. He said it is in the most temperate climate on the East Coast—"a solid zone 7 winter hardiness combined with a heat zone index of one." Before I was bitten by the horticulture bug, Barbara and I traveled to Nantucket, and as soon as we stepped off the boat the lacecap hydrangeas jumped out at us. They made a lasting impression that is still vivid in our minds today. Condon concluded his talk by saying, "We are committed to being stewards of the genus!"

I enjoyed Church because his first book on hydrangeas was my first book on the subject before Dirr appeared on the hydrangea scene. Church has since written a second book on the genus. Dirr has given me several of Church's books, and without exception these contain the best photography of any horticulture book I have ever seen. Barbara and I have visited New Zealand and found it to be one of a few places we wanted to return to from our many travels. Church said the climate in New Zealand could "possibly be the best climate in the world for *Hydrangea macrophylla*." Church's nursery is big into cut flowers, and they ship all over the world. He said he is also a fan of *Dichroa*, the evergreen relative of a *Hydrangea* from Nepal, China, and Vietnam, and plans to cross, like Dirr, the two genera. He also made reference to the Taiwan *Hydrangea angustipetala* that Josh

Kardos is using for crosses with *H. macrophylla*. Among my many things to do (my bucket list) is to visit Condon's farm in Nantucket and Church's garden nursery in New Zealand.

While the hydrangea lectures were fun, even more fun was touring the gardens and bonding with the other attendees. The most productive and enthusiastic group of passionate hydrangea people I met attending the conference was a gang of five from the Mid-South Hydrangea Society in Memphis, Tennessee. The officers Linda Orton, Caroline Brown, Linda Lanier, Kennon Hampton, and his wife, Molly, were all in attendance and soaked up the lectures and tours with a vengeance. Caroline Brown's husband, Steve, was on the trip but spent most of the time touring. His enthusiastic tales of his trip to Flanders Field almost caused me to miss the Shamrock Collection tour the next day. Flanders Field is now on my bucket list.

These ladies (plus one token male) from Memphis get things done. They put out a wonderful newsletter, and one issue was devoted to the international conference, which was a great reference source for me. Being assertive, they secured future lecture dates from our international host Luc Balemans, Glyn Church of New Zealand, Dr. Dirr, and the renowned garden radio and TV host Walter Reeves. The list also includes (what in the world am I doing here?!) yours truly!

We visited four spectacular gardens during the conference. The first morning we went to Kalmthout Arboretum near Antwerp. I soon found out this was the home of the late Robert and Jelena de Belder, internationally famous horticulturists. That got my immediate attention when I found out one of my most favorite witch hazels in my garden is named after her. *Hamamelis* ×*intermedia* 'Jelena' blooms in February and produces fragrant, narrow, ribbonlike, coppery orange petals with a touch of yellow. Seeing where this plant got its name stirred my historical curiosity, so I purchased the book *Jelena and Robert de Belder: Generous as Nature Herself* by Diana Adriaenssen and devoured it on some of our long garden bus rides.

I discovered that in 1952, two brothers who were Antwerp diamond dealers and passionate amateur botanists bought Kalmthout, which had been a longtime deserted nursery and garden. The two brothers, George and Robert de Belder, got help in restoring the old grown-over land by Jelena Kovacic, a recent graduate of horticulture from Slovenia. Robert and Jelena soon fell in love, married, and carried out the restoration of Kalmthout, which is regarded as one of the world's most famous arboretums.

In addition to revising the old nursery, they introduced several plant cultivars, such as 'Jelena', which was found during the restoration. They also introduced 'Diane', named after their daughter, which also has a beautiful bronze witch hazel flower. Unfortunately because the leaves persist, the flowers stay hidden. Every time I passed 'Diane' in my garden, I would pick off some leaves trying to expose the flower, which became an exercise in futility. I finally moved her to a less prominent place in the garden.

I was surprised to learn that among other Kalmthout introductions was *Hydrangea paniculata* 'Unique' and 'Pink Diamond'. I have both in my garden, and 'Pink Diamond' is a real winner. Dr. Dirr, who has used 'Pink Diamond' for several crosses, describes the cultivar in his unique way as "sufficient for any plantsperson to salivate" as the showy sepals turn a "rich pink." I suspect it was named 'Diamond' because the brothers were diamond dealers when they first bought the land. Interesting is the fact 'Pinky Winky', one of the best new introductions, is an open pollination (from seeds) of 'Pink Diamond'.

The book ended sadly when the beloved Jelena, who

Hydrangea paniculata Pinky Winky™
Panicle Hydrangea

became the Royal Horticulture Society vice president, died in August 2003 at the age of seventy-eight.

Making those cultivars like 'Jelena' come alive is fun and adds to the joy of learning. Allan Armitage and Linda Copeland enhanced this intellectual delight by providing the industry and horticulture enthusiasts with the book *Legends in the Garden—Who in the World Is Nellie Stevens?* The authors selected forty-six cultivars (including Barbara, me, and the 'Dooley' hydrangea) revealing how those names of people and places came to represent new cultivars. Armitage and Copeland restricted their list of forty-six to American plants because they felt "too little of American garden history has been told." Nevertheless, the *Legends* journey is pleasant and I refer to the book often.

They start with one of the most beloved and famous hydrangeas 'Annabelle'. How it got its name is a delightful story, as are so many others in the book. The late Professor J. C. McDaniel, horticulture professor at the University of

Hydrangea macrophylla 'Dooley'

Illinois, an interesting character and plant introducer extraordinaire, described the history of 'Annabelle' in a report to the International Plant Propagators Society meeting in December 1962. He found the plant in Urbana, Illinois, but traced it back to Anna, Illinois, where two sisters had seen the plant as far back as 1910. Thus in honor of the "belles of Anna," Illinois, it was called 'Annabelle'.

The Kalmthout Arboretum was so interesting and full of famous cultivars that it was hard to corral the group for lunch, which was cut short to stay on schedule. After lunch the entourage was off to Destelbergen to visit Hydrangeum, the home of the Belgian Hydrangea Society. I was blown away with their collection of over 150 different specimens maintained in a spectacular demonstration garden, and over 600 hydrangea cultivars. It was a memorable sight to see the participants running from plant to plant taking pictures of never-before-seen cultivars of *Hydrangea macrophylla*, *H. paniculata*, *H. quercifolia*, *H. aspera*, and *H. heteromalla*. All of these specimens were in bloom, displaying various shades of color.

What really got my attention and the attention of many of the others was the huge flowers of some of new cultivars of *Hydrangea paniculata*. I was familiar with one called

'Limelight', that was given to me by Allan Armitage a few years ago. It has done marvelously well in the garden. The large inflorescence held high with strong stems makes for a good show, and as the flowers fade it turns to a lime green. However, I was not familiar with 'Phantom' (world's largest *H. paniculata* flower head), 'Big Ben', and 'Silver Dollar', all with white massive flowers standing erect on strong stems. Another new one for me was 'Pinky Winky' with half pink, half white inflorescences, but I now have one in my garden thanks to my friend Mike Sikes of McCorkle Nursery who was also on the trip. I was intrigued with 'Pinky Winky' certainly an attention getter but unusual for sure. I found out the name was derived from a character from a popular children's program a few years ago called *Teletubbies*.

I also secured a few other new *Hydrangea paniculata* that have hit the market from my friend David Shaddix of Hannah's Nursery in Birmingham. I have them planted in the garden in front of the house. I will be watching with interest 'Quickfire', a cultivar that blooms about a month before all the other *H. paniculata*. I will also be watching 'Little Lamb', a compact small-flowered cultivar that I planted next to the creek. I finally secured 'Silver Dollar' a large-flower cultivar that had been difficult to find, and planted it next to the creek. It was blooming away in mid-October and attracted the attention of Dirr who was leading a tour at the time. The *Hydrangea paniculata* species has evidently been underused in the past, but the new cultivars are reversing that trend. I like them all!

SHAMROCK HYDRANGEA GARDEN:
THE NATIONAL HYDRANGEA GARDEN
OF FRANCE

On the last day of the conference we bussed almost four hours, crossing the French border to visit the world-famous Shamrock Hydrangea Garden, officially designated as the National Garden of France for Hydrangea. Corinne and Robert Mallet began developing the garden in 1984, and it now contains over 2,000 hydrangea plants covering over 1,200 different species and cultivars. To my surprise the 'Dooley' hydrangea was among the vast collection.

When I was introduced to Mr. Mallet, he immediately responded, "Mr. Dooley, what a pleasure to meet you, and I want you to see your hydrangea in our collection." We then posed together for a few pictures. I got a real kick out of being famous in France and recognized by a noble Frenchman all because Dr. Dirr named a hydrangea after me.

Mr. Mallet, grandson of Guillaume Mallet, inherited the famous estate known as the Bois des Moutiers, which is located in Varengeville-sur-Mer near Dieppe in upper Normandy. The estate was designed in 1898, and the thirty-acre home, park, and garden that extends all the way to the English Channel is spectacular. We toured the extensive formal walled gardens and the wide paths of the woodlands, marveling at the colossal size of azaleas, rhododendron, and hydrangeas. One plant in particular, among the many that grabbed my attention, was a blue azalea 'les azalea' (*Rhododendron augustinii*). There were many other fascinating plants, but this was a hydrangea trip, so we soon moved on to the five-acre hydrangea shamrock collection while Corrine Mallet led a tour for the Japanese delegate. Robert led the rest of us through the shamrock collection in the rain. The constant downpour did not phase a soul. We moved from one row of hydrangeas to another in the mud with a multitude of "wows!" along the way in different languages. The sizes of the plants and flowers were astounding! No doubt the soil, aided by ideal weather conditions, has allowed this incredible collection to reach its full potential.

The main part of the collection was in a maze where each bed is dedicated to a plant breeder and is arranged according to the continent and/or country. After the tour we toasted our host and hostess and took pictures before boarding the bus home. The four-hour trip back was a pleasure as I got to visit with some of the most respected nursery and plantspeople and horticulture enthusiasts that I've ever met during the course of my horticulture journey.

My Athens buddy, Mark Griffith, who is Dirr's business partner, made the trip along with Rick Crowder, one of the finest nurserymen and nicest people I have met. Rick manages Hawksridge Nursery in Hickory, North Carolina, and many of the specimen plants of the campus statue garden came from there. There is no nursery couple more respected than Linda and J. Guy of Carolina Nurseries, Inc., in Moncks Corner, South Carolina. Meeting for evening libations and dinner in Ghent and listening to all of these passionate plantspeople and soaking up the knowledge made the entire experience extraordinary.

The one person I gained the most respect for was Luc Balemans, who organized the international conference and whose pleasant personality kept everyone in a good mood and on schedule. A visit back to Ghent to see Luc is another trip on my bucket list. When Luc found a way to squeeze me in after the conference was closed (at Dirr's request) he e-mailed me and said to bring some cuttings of 'Dooley'. Being naive, I thought he was kidding until I met him and he asked if I brought any cuttings! Embarrassed I told him I did not, but I shall return one day with some 'Dooley' cuttings. I will tie it in with my trip to Flander's Field.

CHAPTER SIX

STUDIES AT HOME

SEE AMERICA FIRST

My horticulture studies abroad have been educationally exciting and personally rewarding. However, basic education should start at home, and there are some fascinating places to see with marvelous study opportunities right here in the good ol' USA.

I recall a Georgia tourist promotion many years ago aimed at capturing the flood of travelers rushing to Florida that said "See Georgia First." Borrowing from that theme, I have taken every opportunity to see America first. While not as rich in history as our Asian and European counterparts, there are many magnificent and diverse gardens here at home.

An excellent reference book on gardens of the world that I keep handy is entitled *1,001 Gardens You Must See before You Die*. It is a superb book, but the author is British, so naturally there is an extra heavy dose of English gardens, though with good justification. Besides, to the author's credit, he gathered some seventy horticulture experts to help assemble the list of 1,001. So far I have seen 301, which leaves me 700 to go. If I am going to see them all, I'd better pick up the pace and hopefully one day join the centenarian club.

Liriodendron tulipifera 'Tennessee Gold'
Tulip poplar

Cladrastis kentukea
Yellowwood

Ginkgo biloba
Ginkgo

The book does contain 104 magnificent gardens in the United States; though there are dozens more that could have been added. Nevertheless, I have seen about forty of these American gardens listed in the book, and I have many more on my bucket list to see in the future. It is not practical to list all I have visited, but a sprinkling of some of the garden highlights that have made some lasting impressions is worth a journey.

THE NORTHEAST

NEW YORK

The New York Botanical Garden, inspired by the Royal Botanical Gardens in Kew, England, contains the largest conservatory in the country and a herbarium that is one of the largest in the world. But what made an indelible mark on my mind was a magnificent double row of twenty-four tulip poplars (*Liriodendron tulipifera*) that frame the front of the garden library. These stately upright specimens, some over a hundred feet tall, lit up the sky with the brilliant yellow fall color when I was there.

While in the city I also visited Wave Hill Gardens, where at one time Theodore Roosevelt, Mark Twain, and Arturo Toscanini all lived. The estate, with marvelous views of the Hudson River from its 500-foot-high palisades, is breathtaking. There was much to see, but what stands out in my mind is an awesome deciduous tree, which I could not identify, thirty feet tall and wide, completely covered with fruit in a golden appearance accentuated by the sun. After much research it turned out to be the somewhat rare, fragrant Epaulette tree (*Pterostyrax hispida*). I planted one, but after ten years of it not producing fruit and causing space problems, I gave up. I later found out that I could have waited forty years and it never would have produced fruit. The Epaulette tree is dioecious, requiring a male tree to pollinate the female in order to produce fruit. I had space problems with one tree, so you can imagine what two of those trees would have done to the garden. Live and learn—the horticulture education of a football coach continues. Meanwhile, I am content to live with the striking image of the yellow fruit that covered the entire tree on that sunny day in December.

PHILADELPHIA

Farther down the East Coast, just outside of Philadelphia,

Syringa pubescens subsp. *patula* 'Miss Kim'
Manchurian Lilac

Syringa ×*laciniata*
Cutleaf Lilac

is the Bartram Garden, regarded as the oldest botanical garden in America, dated to 1720. It was not easy to find, but because of its historical significance I persisted and was greatly rewarded. The plant-hunting travels of John and his son, William, are legendary. His house is still standing, along with several trees that date from the eighteenth century.

One of the oldest is a magnificent yellowwood (*Cladrastis kentukea*) that dates around 1790. I have two in my garden, and they are handsome specimens producing white, fragrant, drooping flowers in the spring and beautiful yellow fall color.

Bartram's garden also has a *Ginkgo biloba* that is estimated to have been planted around 1785. The highlight is the Franklin tree (*Franklinia alatamaha*), saved from extinction by John Bartram after its discovery in 1765 in south Georgia by the Altamaha River.

BOSTON

Even farther up the East Coast in Boston is the Arnold Arboretum, where I spent a full day but needed a full week to cruise the more than 14,000 plants in the garden. My timing was such that the masses of lilacs (*Syringa* species) throughout the garden were in bloom, and the delightful fragrance that filled the air has never before or since been duplicated in my travels.

It is estimated that there are over twenty different species, and all seemed to have been dispersing their pleasant scent at the same time. They do not perform well as a whole in the heat and humidity of the Deep South, except for the Manchurian lilac (*Syringa pubescens* subspecies *patula* 'Miss Kim' and *Syringa laciniata*). 'Miss Kim' has been a great performer each year in my garden.

While in Boston, I could not pass up the Mount Auburn Cemetery in Cambridge, founded in 1831. There is a self-guided audio driving tour that describes the historic landscape and some of the more than 5,000 trees and 700 species that encompass it.

CALIFORNIA

A few years ago on a trip out to the West Coast I conducted a three-day garden marathon to take in some of the most famous gardens. I started north of San Diego with the mission of San Juan Capistrano (listed as one of the 1,001) for no other reason than I wanted to see where the "swallows came back to Capistrano." I was a little early for the famous birds, since the official traditional day to celebrate the swallows' return to their springtime home is March 19—St. Joseph's Feast day. I have the trip on my bucket list, and if I can ever work it in, Barbara will be with me since March 19 is our anniversary.

I must admit I spent most of my time studying the history (which I enjoy) of the Spanish missions rather then enjoying the beautiful gardens of Capistrano. Next time I will pay more attention to the "garden jewel of the California missions."

My history curiosity continued as I traveled to the J. Paul Getty Villa and Museum outside Los Angeles on the Pacific Palisades. The villa and gardens offer spectacular views of the Pacific Ocean. They also provide a classic example of what can be done with unlimited financial resources. The billionaire philanthropist Getty has turned the magnificent villa into an "ancient Mediterranean world," providing an enlightening experience on how "gardens were integral to Roman life" and what that civilization "and the Greeks and Etruscans contributed to our gardening heritage."

While in the LA area I took in the Huntington Botanical Garden. The 150-acre garden area features classical Japanese and Chinese gardens, as well as a desert garden of some 4,000 species.

Drought-tolerant plants, however, are best demonstrated in the Ruth Bancroft Garden in Walnut Creek outside of San Francisco. The garden has an incredible succulent and cactus collection thanks to Miss Ruth, who is recognized worldwide as a leader in water-conserving plants. While touring the garden I stumbled upon Ruth Bancroft, at the age of ninety-five (she is one hundred as of this writing), who was squatting down and working in the garden. I will never forget that remarkable scene. She was extremely pleasant and hospitable, and we had a

Aesculus parviflora
Bottlebrush Buckeye

nice conversation about gardening, contrasting the East and West Coasts.

Visiting with Miss Ruth has always been an inspiring and memorable moment in my horticulture journey.

MISSOURI BOTANICAL: A FAVORITE

One of my most favorite gardens is the Missouri Botanical in St. Louis, recognized as the oldest formal botanical garden in the United States. I have been there on two occasions, once with my brother, Billy Dooley, a successful former college football coach and administrator who started his career with me here at Georgia. We were in St. Louis on Olympic business in 1994 in preparation for the 1996 Centennial Olympics in Atlanta. The scene most vivid in my mind was the large mass of bottlebrush buckeyes (*Aesculus parviflora*) that were in bloom. I immediately thought of Dr. Dirr, who loves the plant so much he told me it ought to be designated as the *national* shrub! I got him on the phone and had fun sharing the flowering buckeye scene that got him excited.

I returned to the garden in 2009 while on a Civil War tour. It was perfect timing as the garden was celebrating its

150th birthday. I purchased a beautiful sesquicentennial book published that year that succinctly describes the history of the botanical garden started by philanthropist Henry Shaw in 1859.

To my surprise I learned that the Missouri Botanical Garden is part of a "global community of over 2,500 botanical gardens." I also learned that these gardens are unified, sharing the same mission to "collect, preserve, and display plants for beauty, scientific research, and education. Most contain living collections of plants, as one would expect, but also libraries and collections of dried plants known as herbaria. They are parks, laboratories, classrooms, and living museums of natural history rolled into one. They are refuges for beleaguered urbanites seeking the restorative peace found in plants and the natural world." I found this to be an excellent definition of the often-asked question: What is a botanical garden?

I like the Missouri Botanical Garden because every part of the fifty-plus acres is enjoyable. It is beautiful, historic, and spacious, but compact enough that two laps around the garden leaves you with the feeling you want to take a third. That is especially true of the fourteen-acre Japanese garden billed as the "largest Japanese stroll garden in the West."

While strolling I found another must-have plant, a Japanese red pine (*Pinus densiflora*). I have two cultivars 'Aurea' and 'Oculus-draconis' (Dragon Eye) that provide striking yellow color, but this cultivar 'Umbraculifera' got my attention with its brilliant red orange bark.

I could go on about the garden, but before leaving I should mention the George Washington Carver Sculpture Garden, which honors the life and accomplishments of a Missourian who overcame great prejudice to become "one of the nation's foremost agricultural scientists and educational innovators." He was known as the father of the peanut industry.

Pinus densiflora 'Burke's Red Variegated'
Japanese Red Pine

THE LOW COUNTRY

Since I grew up in Mobile, Alabama, I have always had an affection for the low country region of the South. Even though I have lived away from the coast since I finished high school, I get nostalgic whenever I am around the tidal waters. I enjoy bayous, lagoons, rivers, and bays and the surrounding live oaks (*Quercus virginiana*) and hanging Spanish moss (*Tillandsia* spp.)

There are so many beautiful low-country plantations and gardens, it is almost impossible to know where to start or end. However, Bellingrath Garden, outside of Mobile, Alabama, provides a good starting point. Growing up I always heard about the garden but never had any special desire to visit it, nor the resources, as a Great Depression youngster, to gain admittance. It was not until I returned to the area ten years later with my young bride, Barbara, from Birmingham, that I visited the garden. I have been back several times since.

The garden started out in 1918 as a fishing bungalow on Fowl River for Walter Bellingrath, who made millions through the Coca-Cola bottling franchises in the largest cities in Alabama. With the initiative of his wife, Bessie, the property ended up being the most magnificent floral display garden in the South and certainly the best such garden I have ever seen. There are seemingly endless displays of rows and rows of flowers showing the colors of the different seasons. The highlight is the azalea display that is probably unmatched anywhere else in the country. Can you imagine 250,000 azalea plants blooming in springtime? Just as impressive are the 60,000 chrysanthemums blooming in November. Whatever the season, the colorful displays are awesome.

THE SOUTH CAROLINA LOW COUNTRY

I have visited two old plantation-style gardens (Magnolia Gardens and Middleton Place), both located on the Ashley River, close to Charleston, that stand out in my memory. Both are historic sites dating from pre-Revolutionary War times, yet contrasting in style. Middleton Place has been described as "sedate, cultured, and aristocratic," while Magnolia Gardens is "feisty and free and is in touch with the times."

What struck me at Middleton Place was the view from the plantation house of the wide-open, green, terraced lawn as it sweeps down to two butterfly-shaped lakes near the Ashley River. This spectacular sense of formality and grace was the ideal backdrop for the unforgettable setting in the movie *The Patriot* starring Mel Gibson, who played General Francis Marion, "the Swamp Fox." During the Revolutionary War, Marion carried on guerrilla warfare against the invading British Redcoats who had captured Charleston. The ceremonial scene shows British general Cornwallis dressed in royal regalia welcoming the many dignitaries to the party on the spacious terraced lawn by the lakes and river. "The Swamp Fox" threw a monkey wrench in the extravaganza by blowing up a British ship on the river. However, the explosion did

add to the spectacular beauty of the grand occasion by lighting up the skies.

1,001 Gardens pays homage to the ancient live oak (estimated at 1,000 years) at the entrance of the grounds and calls Middleton Place "the oldest extant garden in the United States."

The 500-acre Magnolia Garden, just a few miles from Middleton Place, did not make the cut of *1,001 Gardens*. They should have added Magnolia Garden and named the book *1,002 Gardens You Must See before You Die*. Magnolia Plantation Garden is delightful both for its historical significance and its year-round garden attraction.

The garden was established in 1679 by Thomas Drayton. In the more than 330 years since its beginning, it has stayed in the Drayton family, with each succeeding generation responsible for its welfare. Through the years each owner has kept pace with the times, meeting the challenge to keep the garden intact. Today, both the thirteenth and fourteenth generations are continuing the tradition of excellence that has been passed to them.

In 1825, at the tender age of twenty-two, John Drayton became the fifth generation to inherit the plantation. Despite the wealth and prestige he inherited, he vowed to pursue his goal to be a minister and was ordained an Episcopalian priest in New York. Returning to the South Carolina low country, he devoted himself to the enhancement of the plantation and became the rector of nearby Saint Andrew Church.

Reverend Drayton changed the emphasis of the garden from the formal design borrowed from the French to embellishing the natural beauty of the site in a manner prevalent in England at the time. He introduced the first azaleas to America and was one of the first to utilize *Camellia japonica* in an outdoor setting. Today there are over 900 varieties of camellias in the garden.

The Civil War threatened the welfare of the plantation

Camellia japonica

I would be remiss not to at least mention Barbara's and my visit a few years ago to the plantation homes and gardens along the Mississippi River. Before the Civil War, when cotton was king, Natchez, Mississippi, was a city of millionaires. Thanks to a lot of civic pride and especially the garden clubs in Natchez, many of the magnificent plantation homes and gardens have been preserved. We spent a delightful two days there with a promise to return.

The area just north of Baton Rouge on the Mississippi River that surrounds the city of St. Francisville was, like Natchez, a land of beautiful plantations and gardens. There are only a few left, with the grand plantation home and garden of Rosedown being the crème de la crème. The mansion and garden provide a spectacular glimpse of life in the antebellum South. The home is framed with a long allèe of live oaks, most over 200 years old. The garden has been completely restored, thanks to Mrs. Catherine Underwood, who purchased the plantation in 1956.

My main reason for going to St. Francisville was to see Afton Villa, another restored garden that has been built around the ruins of the plantation house that burned to the ground in 1963. I had met the owner, Genevieve (Jan) Trimble, and her late husband, Morrill Trimble, who restored the garden, through our friends Vernon and Patricia Brinson while in New Orleans when our team was there for the Sugar Bowl in 2002. A visit with Jan Trimble sparked my interest, and we arranged for a visit and garden tour while we were in Baton Rouge to see our son Derek, who at the time was coaching at LSU.

When we arrived at the garden, a deluge had swamped the area, but Jan with a yellow raincoat, hat, and umbrella, and me with an umbrella, enthusiastically toured the garden while Barbara stayed inside with Jan's daughter, Morrill. I loved Mrs. Trimble's spirit and enthusiasm, and

and the family. Two of John Drayton's nephews fought against each other in the war, ironically, in the Battle of Hilton Head, not far from the Drayton estate. Confederate General Thomas Drayton and Union Admiral Percival Drayton, brothers, were assigned responsible positions in the battle. General Drayton was in charge in the defense of Hilton Head and its earthworks, while Admiral Drayton was in charge of one of the attacking Federal gunboats. Both survived the war, only to see the family plantation ravaged by the conflict and on the verge of collapse.

Uncle John Drayton saved the garden by opening it up to the public in 1872, making the garden "the first man-made tourist attraction in the United States." Since that time the garden has evolved and grown to become the last surviving nineteenth-century romantic garden of its size in the United States, as well as one of the greatest public gardens in America.

we had a marvelous time moving about despite the drenching rain that never eased up. Jan was especially proud of the "ruined garden," as it is affectionately called. That area is where the steps, foundations, stones, and a partial brick wall remain. The "ruined garden" is sprinkled with container plants resting under some tall stately trees that gracefully droop over the area.

After about an hour and a half we returned drenched but happy, to the astonishment of Barbara and Morrill, who just shook their heads. My response was, "It never rains on the practice field or in the garden."

On the same trip, we stopped at the home of Robert E. "Buddy" Lee in Independence, Louisiana. Buddy developed the Encore® (reblooming) azalea that has lit up the market. I was expecting to find an elaborate high-tech greenhouse and garden; instead Barbara and I found a very modest home and azalea garden compatible with this humble gentleman. Buddy is in much demand as a speaker, so I often see him at nursery shows. Every time I see extensive advertisement and promotion of the Encore® azalea, I think of Buddy Lee and his small azalea garden where it all began in the early 1980s.

GEORGIA: IN THE ZONE

Georgia is the largest state east of the Mississippi and the only one in that half of the country that contains (just barely) four hardiness zones. The northern parts of Rabun, Townes, Union, and Fannin counties in northeast Georgia are in zone 6b. The rest of the state is divided between 7a and b and 8a and b, except for a small portion of the southeast (Camden and Glynn counties) that is zone 9a. How does an area get in a particular zone and what does it mean? In the midfifties the Department of Agriculture (USDA) mapped the United States, Mexico, and Canada by the lowest annual minimum temperature into eleven zones. Each zone represents a 10-degree-Fahrenheit difference. The maps have been revised over the years with the latest revision in 1990 including the numbered zones broken down to a and b. In Athens we are 7b, which indicates an average winter minimum temperature of 10 degrees to 5 degrees Fahrenheit.

After gathering this information, I got curious about Georgia having four zones and also about the average temperature minimum in Athens. I have often said that one of the great advantages of living around a university is that you can satisfy any curiosity because there is an expert on everything. So I picked up the phone and called my friend, Dr. David Stooksbury, who is an engineering professor at the university and a state climatologist. Dr. Stooksbury confirmed that Georgia has four zones, referring to the mountains and to the area right along the coast east of I-95 that account for the 6b and 9a extreme zones respectively. He also confirmed the average winter temperature in Athens is between 10 and 5 degrees Fahrenheit, stating that more than likely one night during the winter it will drop that low. He also stated, to my complete surprise, it could go lower, which he said it did in January 1985 when it dropped to negative 3 degrees Fahrenheit, a record low here in Athens. I have no recollection of it ever getting that cold in Athens, but then again I was still coaching and unaware of a lot of things going on at that time. After visiting with Dr. Stooksbury and satisfying my curiosity, I found the USDA is at it again. They have now added to the eleven—zones 12–15 include Hawaii and Puerto Rico—as well as better details for tropical plants.

The system is a good tool for gardeners to evaluate geographical limits of plant adaptability, but it is far from the final word. There are lots of marginal-zone adaptable plants, and only by trial and error can it be determined if certain plants can thrive in a particular zone. For instance, in Rabun County (zone 6b) where we have a house on Lake

Hibiscus chinensis 'Mutablis'
Confederate Rose

Burton, the Fraser magnolia (*Magnolia fraseri*) thrives and can grow to sixty feet. I brought one home, planted it in the garden, and carefully nursed it for four years. It languished and I don't believe it grew an inch in that time before finally kicking the bucket. The magnolia was not a happy camper, though it might have done better in another place in the garden if I had moved it. On reflection I should have, and since that time I have moved every unhappy plant.

Similarly while in St. Simons (zone 9a) I identified this twenty-foot tree that was loaded with red-to-pink peony-type flowers in September as a Confederate Rose (*Hibiscus chinensis* 'Mutablis'). I had visions of this beautiful flowering tree in my garden so I took several cuttings and planted them in the yard and some on the farm in Madison County. They all prospered and bloomed the first year, which excited me. However, when winter came I was introduced to the term *die back*. In our 7b zone, the Confederate Rose is a die-back plant that disappears in the winter, grows rapidly in the summer, and blooms in late September and October before dying back again in the winter. Confident that I had evaluated the Confederate Rose's adaptability to our zone, I found an exception. Some twenty miles from Athens, in Lexington, Georgia, is

the renowned Goodness Grows retail nursery run by my friend Rick Berry. In his garden area there is a Confederate Rose that never dies back and is happy all year. Every time I visit Goodness Grows, I ask Rick why his plant prospers year-round and mine does not. He just smiles, throws his arms in the air, and says, "I don't know!" I don't know either, but I do know it's not just the cold factor that affects plants; it's the heat factor as well. Most people know, and I have learned, that extreme cold kills plants instantly, while plant death from heat is slow and lingering. Since heat is an important issue in plant survival, the American Horticulture Society introduced a plant heat zone map in 1997. The map divides the country into twelve zones and assigns numbers to sections of the country based on a particular region's average number of days it experiences "heat days," defined as temperatures over 86 degrees Fahrenheit.

At the International Hydrangea Conference, Mal Condon spoke about his New England home on Nantucket Island as being an ideal place to grow hydrangeas. I remembered he said it is because the area is "a solid zone 7 winter hardiness combined with a heat zone index of 1." At the time I didn't know what a heat zone was but I figured a 1 must really be good. The fact is, a 1 is the best and means that the average number of days per year the temperature gets over 86 degrees is only one day. Contrast this with zone 11 in the southern parts of Florida, Texas, and Arizona, where the average number of days over 86 degrees annually is 180–210. Here in Athens, Georgia, we are an 8, indicating on average there will be 90–100 days where the temperature rises above 86 degrees.

Despite all the good works done by the USDA and the American Horticulture Society to better measure plants' ability to survive cold and hot temperatures, the systems still remain imperfect. It will never be foolproof as long as there are a variety of factors—early fall and late spring freezes, night temperatures, day length, light, elevation,

humidity, rainfall, and cultivar-hardiness variations—that influence the growth of plants. Therefore, reliance on information from those passionate plantspeople that have dedicated themselves to evaluation and research has become increasingly more important, and my appreciation of their efforts grows with each season.

COX ARBORETUM

No one is appreciated more in this regard than Tom Cox and his supportive wife, Evelyn, who for the past two decades have devoted themselves to collecting, preserving, and evaluating plants and trees from around the world in their zone 7b arboretum.

Tom is a fellow Alabamian, but unlike me he grew up around a garden and developed early on a joy of learning about plants and trees. After retiring from the military he met his wife while working for BellSouth in Atlanta, and she became his number-one supporter of his horticulture passion. Tom and Evelyn started an arboretum in 1990 from fourteen acres that they had earlier bought to build a home near Canton, Georgia. While Tom obsessed with learning everything he could about trees and plants, he became, like me and many others, a Dr. Dirr disciple. We both were beneficiaries of Dirr's appreciation of those who are infected by the horticulture disease. Tom told me when he first attended conferences as an unknown, feeling somewhat isolated, Dirr would wave him over to join the crowd that was always gathered around the horticulture guru. Tom always appreciated Dirr for that inclusion, calling him the person who helped him the most. Dirr admired Cox's persistence and called him "phenomenal—he's chasing the latest, greatest, craziest, most unusual trees in the world."

Today the Cox Arboretum has over 4,000 living specimens, displaying one of the largest private collections of temperate flora in the entire United States. Trees are a real passion, and he has over 600 representing some forty countries around the world. Recently Tom was selected as a member of the International Dendrology (study of trees) Society that spans some fifty countries. There are only four members from the United States, and Tom is proud to be in that exclusive body whose mission is "to study, conserve and protect woody plants and shrubs throughout the world."

In conjunction with his passion for trees he developed a special interest in conifers, the cone-bearing woody plants. There are more than 500 species representing some of the smallest, largest, and oldest trees in the world. Following the Cox pattern of persistence he became the first southerner to be elected national president of the society, and Evelyn became the editor of the *Conifer Quarterly*. Today Tom is cowriting a book on conifers of the South with Dr. John Ruter, professor of horticulture research at the University of Georgia on the Tifton campus.

I first met Tom when I toured his arboretum with Dirr a few years after he opened the garden. I had just gotten the bug after taking a few of Dirr's courses and started following him on various road trips. I was a raw but enthusiastic learner as I followed Tom and Dirr, trying to absorb their horticultural dialogue as we walked from one plant and tree to the next. While I knew little about what was going on, I was observant enough to recall that the arboretum was having growing pains, and I thought to myself it was in much need of maturity. What a difference ten years makes in a garden; I returned a decade later to an absolutely amazing arboretum.

I spent that entire day getting a one-on-one tour from Tom who, like me, enjoys not only the plants and trees but their history. I was taking notes as fast as I could, picking up some educational gems from Tom. I was aware that the common feature of most all conifers is that they produce cones. The word *conifer* means in Latin "to bear cones." I

Taxodium distichum 'Cascade Falls', fall color
Weeping Baldcypress

Metasequoia glyptostroboides
Dawn Redwood

was not aware, however, that there are exceptions: for example, junipers that produce fleshy, berrylike cones and yews that produce a naked seed with a fleshy covering.

Tom further mentioned there were five conifers that are deciduous. I was aware of four and have them in my garden. The first is the baldcypress (*Taxodium distichum*) and next is a close relative, the dawn redwood (*Metasequoia glyptostroboides*). They can be hard to tell apart, but thanks to Dirr's course I was able to answer Tom's question in that regard. The leaves of the baldcypress are alternate, while the dawn redwood leaves are opposite. The third deciduous conifer is the *Larix*, or larch, and I have a weeping form by the creek. Last is the golden larch (*Pseudolarix amabilis*), regarded as the golden coin tree in China, and I somehow ended up with three in the garden.

I was not familiar with the fifth deciduous conifer, a Chinese swamp cypress (*Glyptostrobus pensilis*) believed to bring good luck in China. It is rare in all of China except in the river delta in Guandong Province. *Glyptostrobus pensilis* is the only species in the genus, and I rather suspect in time the small tree that produces cypress knees will become extinct one day.

Some conifers are hard to distinguish from others, but Tom pointed out a good key to identify a falsecypress (*Chamaecyparis*). He showed me the backside of the leaf that is identified by tiny white Xs (in some cases Ys); upon close observation they are recognizable, and this key is a tremendous help since there are some five falsecypress species representing hundreds of cultivars.

While we were discussing conifers I got an additional education on one of my most favorite trees, a Deodar or Himalayan cedar (*Cedrus deodara*). It is a graceful tree, and I like the hand-grenade-looking erect cones produced noticeably in the upper branches of the trees. I observed that Tom had a cedar where the branches almost touch the ground, and I could see multitudes of

Chamaecyparis obtuse
Hinoki Falsecypress

Cedrus libani
Cedar of Lebanon

Abies firma
Momi Fir

pinky-finger-size cones that I assumed would grow up to be the hand-grenade cones in time. I revealed my ignorance and Tom enlightened me that the small cones on the bottom were the male cones that would send up a cloud of yellow pollen to pollinate the female cones. The cedar is monoecious, meaning that on the same tree or plant there are male and female reproductive organs in separate structures. It was fun to pick up this tidbit, and the next day, driving by a beautiful Deodora cedar by the house, I noticed the multitude of male cones on the lower branches and smiled with my new knowledge, looking forward to the fall when they will send up their cloud of yellow pollen.

Tom was filling me with a lot of knowledge and I had little to give back, except when we were discussing the cedars of Lebanon (*Cedrus libani*). Since Barbara is third-generation Lebanese, we traveled the country a few years ago. She was in pursuit of her heritage, and I was in pursuit of the cedars of Lebanon—a tree that at one time covered almost the entire country. Today there are few left except for a cluster preserved on top of a mountain in a national forest in the Cedars of Lebanon region. Our Athens friend Tony Salloum, a native of Lebanon, was our escort and took us up to the town of Bicharia to see those magnificent trees. I mentioned it to Tom, and I believe that is the only place in the world he has not been to observe the great trees of the world. That might also be true of my many mentors, including Dr. Dirr.

Tom did mention the Bedgebury National Pinetum in England, explaining that *pinetum* did not refer to pines but to a collection of conifers. He asked me if I had ever been to see this collection of over 10,000 trees and shrubs—the most complete collection of temperate conifers in the world. I was on a roll at that point and answered yes. I told him I had been there with Dr. Dirr several years ago and saw a Leyland cypress (×*Cupressocyparis leylandii*) that was 130 feet tall. Tom was pleased with my response. I didn't contribute much after that during our tour but thoroughly enjoyed Tom pointing out plants and trees (and an occasional horticulture oddity) and throwing in some historical points of interest.

At that point Tom excused himself to meet with an electrician who had come to check the irrigation system that had been struck by lightning the previous night. This gave me a chance to reflect on the pinetum discussion, which reminded me of the University of Georgia's state arboretum in Jackson County, near Braselton, called Thompson Mills Forest. The arboretum features a pinetum that contains all the native conifers of Georgia and more than a hundred species of gymnosperms from twenty-seven countries. The enthusiastic keeper of the 318-acre arboretum, Bill Lott, has given me several tours of this state educational laboratory. Meanwhile, Tom returned and we continued our tour of the Cox Arboretum.

We passed an Osage-orange tree (*Maclura pomifera*) and Tom called it "bois d'arc," explaining that the French expression means "bow of the wood," since the Indians used the rot-resistant tree to make bows. The best bows are still made from the wood today. The tree was also used in the United States as a hedgerow and that use was a factor in the Civil War battle of Franklin, Tennessee, a Confederate disaster late in the war. There also is a colony of Osage-orange trees in the Barnsley Garden Resort near Adairsville, Georgia. I saw them there several years ago, which prompted my search to identify these trees with their huge orange-like fruit. The search unfolded an interesting history centered around the Osage Indians of the lower Midwest plains.

Tom then pointed to a tung oil tree (*Vernicia fordii*), stating that Henry Ford once planted it in groves in Florida to extract furniture oil from the seed pods. It is still used today in the paint and varnish industry.

We passed a couple of Snowbells, the first a *Styrax japonicus* called 'Emerald Pagoda' that he called the late Dr. J. C. Raulston's "greatest contribution to horticulture." The newest *Styrax* Tom is excited about is from Taiwan (China) called *Styrax formosanus*, which blooms earlier than any in the genus. He is also excited about his maple from China (*Acer pentaphyllum*) that he explained was the rarest maple on Earth. Another interesting maple we passed was a striped snakebark maple. I remember I had gotten one from Dirr but forgot the species. When I got home I checked and found I have an *Acer capillipes*, one of fourteen Asiatic snakebark maples, the same species Tom has in the arboretum. The green bark, with light green and red brown stripes, provides year-round interest in my garden. I also acquired another snakebark cultivar *Acer tegmentosum* from Mildred Fockele, director of horticulture at the Atlanta Botanical Garden.

At the start of the walk next to the house, Tom pointed out the Wollemi pine (*Wollemia nobilis*) a new introduction from Australia that he is evaluating for growth adaptability in the South. What got my attention were the numerous dwarf *Ginkgo biloba* he was evaluating. He has at least ten varieties of this fascinating tree whose history dates back over 150 million years. Because my 'Witch's Broom' dwarf ginkgo has performed well, I am anxious to follow the evaluation of Tom's dwarf selections.

I was also impressed with the work Tom is doing crossing *Abies firma* (Japanese fir), the amazing heat-tolerant fir, with several other firs that do not hold up in the South. His conclusion is that any cross with the heat-tolerant *Abies firma* will produce spectacular heat-tolerant firs.

The list of plants in the Cox Arboretum goes on and on. Tom's collection of redbuds (*Cercis* species) got my attention also, along with a must-have weeping parrotia,

Styrax japonicus 'Emerald Pagoda'
Japanese Snowbell

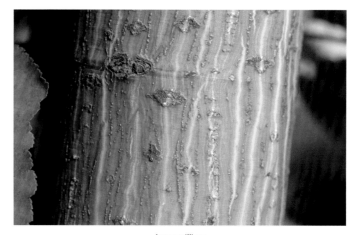

Acer capillipes
Snakebark Maple

assuming I can find room on "weepers creek" in the garden.

The industry will long be indebted to Tom for the work he has done at his arboretum. He calls it his legacy—he explains, "Some people leave books. I leave trees!"

ARMITAGE AND DIRR: THE GOLDEN YEARS

The years 1980–83 were the golden era for football at the University of Georgia. During those four years, the team record was 43-4-1, the best of any program in the country. Those teams won three Southeastern Conference championships and a national championship and participated in four major bowl games.

At about the same time the Department of Horticulture at the University of Georgia was embarking on its golden years. Two professors of horticulture, Dr. Allan A. Armitage and Dr. Michael A. Dirr, were hired by the university and both were highly regarded and soon became nationally and internationally world-renowned as teachers, writers, speakers, consultants, and researchers. No institution of higher education in the nation has ever had two more distinguished teaching and research scholars in one discipline than Dr. Armitage and Dr. Dirr. Both have their horticulture

specialty—Dr. Dirr, the woody plant guru; Dr. Armitage, the herbaceous plant guru. Both played major roles in two of the university's greatest assets, the State Botanical Garden of Georgia and the University of Georgia's trial garden. They respect each other and get along well, but they are always kidding each other about their specialty. Somebody quipped that the reason they get along so well is that "Dirr looks up; Armitage looks down!"

THE STATE BOTANICAL GARDEN OF GEORGIA

Dr. Dirr became director of the 313-acre state botanical garden located on the grounds of the University of Georgia in 1979. He served for two years before returning to the university to teach. He laid a solid foundation for the garden that is now regarded as a true gem among public gardens. Dr. Dirr was the moving force to obtain the conservatory building that is the crown jewel of the garden.

I had the privilege of serving on the board of trustees for several years, gaining a real appreciation for the dedicated work done by the staff and the board of trustees. Everyone was in full support of the emphasis placed by the garden on learning. That emphasis has enabled the garden to become a "living laboratory" for faculty, students, and horticulture enthusiasts. I especially was supportive of the garden's emphasis on the study of the history of plants. This resulted in the development of two unique gardens—the international and heritage gardens—both focusing on the role of plants in history. The entire garden is an educational jewel, and living in Athens and around the university is another of the many bonuses the university and the community have to offer.

THE UGA TRIAL GARDENS

The other research laboratory gem of the university's campus is the trial gardens at UGA. Dr. Armitage started it in 1982. He has almost single-handedly grown and developed the garden into one of the best trial gardens in America. His reputation is so widespread that plant breeders from around the world want to test their plants in the UGA trial garden.

Meanwhile the UGA students benefit by being constantly exposed to many varieties of annuals and perennial species. It is an extraordinary opportunity to study the different growth habits, heat tolerance, and uses of so many herbaceous plants.

Dr. Armitage is especially proud of the fact that over the years the garden has reduced its environmental impact by "minimizing water use, maximizing soil nutrients and reducing the use of plastics and letting nature work."

Many plants such as *Verbena* 'Homestead Purple', 'Margarita' sweet potato, and the first-ever sun-loving *Coleus* have come from the trial garden. Today plants originating from the trial garden are marketed under the Athens Select label, a national program, as well as being partnered with *Southern Living* magazine and its branded plants.

Barbara and I have received many benefits from living in the Athens community and around the university, but none more from our association with the Armitages (Allan and Susan) and the Dirrs (Mike and Bonnie) and to reap the rewards of the State Botanical Garden and the university's trial garden where both have left their footprints.

We have grown to love both of these families. We have especially been touched by the heavy cross that the Dirrs carried in their struggles to prolong the life of their daughter, Susy, born with cystic fibrosis. It is a genetic condition that affects the cells living in the lungs and digestive system, causing a wide range of health problems.

Barbara and I were very familiar with the condition. When we lived in Auburn, Alabama, some of our closest friends, Bobbie and Fob James, had a son born with cystic fibrosis. Fob and I had been teammates and roommates at Auburn before he later became the two-time governor of the state. The Jameses were financially capable of giving their son, Greg, the best possible treatment available at the time. However, back then patients typically did not survive childhood. Greg lived longer than most, dying at the age of twelve. Today research has extended the lives of cystic fibrosis patients into the early thirties.

Susy died at thirty-one. Before she succumbed to the disease, her mom and dad had moved to Chapel Hill with Susy to be near the North Carolina Transplant Hospital. Eventually Susy had two lung transplants, each time providing her with a substantially improved quality of life, albeit temporarily.

We agonized with the Dirrs as they suffered through the emotional roller coaster. Susy was an inspiration to all who knew her. Despite her life-and-death struggle, she pressed on to become valedictorian of her high school class and an honor student at the University of Georgia, where she received her degree in journalism. She developed an envious attitude, mixing a good sense of humor with a practical and finally peaceful outlook about her condition. She felt blessed with her family and many friends. She was admired and loved by all who knew her.

When Susy was living in Chapel Hill, Dirr surprisingly discovered a new yellow, cold-hardy (zone 7) seedling of *Lantana* that was growing in her backyard. He named the plant 'Chapel Hill Yellow'. Dirr surmised the discovery was a natural cross between the cold-hardy *Lantana* 'Miss Huff' and the spreading annual *Lantana* 'New Gold'. Afterward and while breeding 'Chapel Hill Yellow' in his Plant Introductions, Inc. company (PII), his partner Mark Griffith discovered a gold sport of the plant. Now there are two new cold-hardy Lantanas 'Chapel Hill Yellow' and 'Chapel Hill Gold'. With the support of the PII Company, the compassionate Mike and Bonnie Dirr have directed a generous portion of the royalties from any *Lantana* sales to the Sweet Melissa Fund. The charity is a nonprofit to raise money for lung-transplant recipients and their families. The fund is named for Melissa Alexander, a friend of Susy's and a cystic fibrosis patient who died during a lung-transplant operation in 2005. Armitage also went out of his way to include the *Lantana* in the trial garden. They are appreciated by all who walk through.

I have both 'Chapel Hill Yellow' and 'Gold' in the perennial gardens behind the house and at the top of the hill next to the entrance to the driveway. They both have been great performers, offering bittersweet memories of sweet Susy, God's gift for thirty-one years to her family and those blessed to have known her.

THE SOUTHEASTERN HORTICULTURE SOCIETY

During the time I was serving on the state botanical board I was approached about serving on the Southeast Flower Show board. It was an offer that was hard to refuse since the flower show president at the time, Diane Fiesta, had the just-retired Archbishop of Atlanta, John Donoghue, call me to arrange a luncheon engagement to ask the ques-

Lantana camara 'Chapel Hill Gold'
Lantana

tion. It was hard to say no to the church hierarchy so I accepted, but felt it was prudent to resign from the state botanical board, especially since I had served the organization for five years. I was anxious to take on a new venture that afforded me an opportunity to serve and increase my horticulture knowledge.

I had fun participating in various activities during the shows each year. I teamed up one year with Dr. Dirr to act as an auctioneer during a fund-raising plant sale. On another occasion I reluctantly agreed, for the good of the cause, to participate in a celebrity flower-arrangement contest. During the contest I was hoping none of my former players or coaches showed up or found out about it. The event drew a nice crowd, and to my astonishment I won the contest, just barely beating my friend Joe Washington, a highly respected public affairs, sports, and landscape broadcaster and a very knowledgeable gardener. It was a major upset, perhaps stimulated by sympathetic judges who appreciated the efforts of a football coach totally devoid of the art of flower arranging.

The flower shows were all outstanding events, well attended with judging taking place in competitive landscape and floral designs. Some of Atlanta's leading landscapers have traditionally gone all-out designing gardens and competing for various awards. I even had an award named after me, the Vince Dooley Showmanship Challenge Award. They call it the "WOW" award, because it is presented for the exhibit that takes a garden to a "WOW" level of fantasy, entertainment, and theater. My friend Ed Castro won in 2010. The criteria were based solely on "wow" reactions from the judges, as opposed to grandiose, elaborate garden designs. I recall two years ago that landscape designer Brooks Garcia of Atlanta Fine Arts Garden won the award with a small seventh-century hermitlike garden. The quaint garden design was dedicated to the patron saint of gardening, St. Fiacre, a seventh-century French monk born in Ireland, who committed himself to a life of prayer and labor in the garden. Barbara was so impressed with the statue of St. Fiacre that was used in the garden display she ordered one for our garden, and it rests in the patio container garden outside the back door.

To broaden the scope of the annual flower show, our visionary president Robert Balentine led the board in forming the Southeastern Horticulture Society. The new organization's mission is to promote year-round "the knowledge, art and enjoyment of horticulture." There are annual events such as lectures, garden tours, and plant sales to supplement the annual flower show, which is the crown jewel event of the society.

Another popular initiative is the legacy garden. This is a garden award developed from some of the resources of the flower show and presented to a nonprofit for the benefit of the needy of a particular charity. For instance, the 2009 legacy garden recipient is Skyland Trail South residential facility, where a therapeutic green space and healing garden were developed to aid in their patients' recovery. The garden is indeed good for the body, mind, heart, and soul, and the newly formed Southeastern Horticulture Society is a strong proponent of those spiritual and physical rewards.

Ed Castro won the 2010 Vince Dooley Showmanship Challenge Award at the Southeastern Flower Show

THE ATLANTA BOTANICAL GARDENS AND CALLAWAY GARDENS: TWO IN GEORGIA OF THE 1,001

The Atlanta Botanical Garden and Callaway Gardens are the only two Georgia gardens listed in the book *1,001 Gardens You Must See before You Die*. I have seen them both on several occasions and even spoken at gardening events at both places.

It is ironic that, despite my novice horticulture background, I get a lot of invitations to speak on gardening. No doubt the novelty of a football coach lecturing on gardening is the main reason, certainly not my horticulture expertise. I was only a two-year letterman in horticulture when I was asked to join Armitage and Dirr to lecture on gardening at a seminar at the Bernheim Arboretum near Louisville, Kentucky. The invitation came from noted horticulturist Paul Cappiello, a former Dirr student and curator of the arboretum at the time. I had gotten to know Paul on our first garden trip with Dirr to England. When Paul invited me to speak I thought he was joking, and still do today.

I found myself again asking the question, "What in the world am I doing here?" I was trying to make excuses about the speaking challenges and my horticulture shortcomings, comparing my speaking on gardening to Armitage and Dirr speaking at a coaching convention. Though I was a little uptight about it at first, I have been on the firing line many times in my coaching career, so I started working on the old "5 Ps," a coaching axiom that states—Proper Preparation Prevents Poor Performance.

I made bundles of notes and had been over them several times, confidently prepared, when low and behold, during my talk the note pages got scrambled and I started to sweat. Knowing I couldn't reconstruct the messed-up notes I called an audible, explained my situation, and winged the rest of the talk. My mentors were complimentary mainly for my courageous effort, but I was happy it was over.

The experience, however, did help my confidence, as many young gardeners in attendance could relate to my experiences. Before long I had more invitations coming my way. After fretting over the invites, most of which were hard to turn down, I finally adopted the Armitage attitude— have fun with it—which is the way gardening should be.

I first acquired the Armitage have-fun attitude while speaking in Asheville, North Carolina, with both Dirr and him. Speaking on gardening was one thing, but once again being sandwiched between these two horticultural professionals was not only ridiculous but downright laughable. I was either going to laugh or cry, so I decided to have fun with it.

Recently Armitage reminded me that on that Asheville speaking engagement, Dirr and he brought a variety of plants they had introduced for a fund-raising sale. He reminded me that since I had not introduced any plants (still haven't), I brought a football I had autographed, and it carried the highest price of the evening. No doubt some passionate gardening lady dragged her football-crazed husband to the horticulture seminar and he ended up buying the football.

I have spoken to numerous garden clubs, mainly in Georgia, and I can tell you it is more fun speaking to an audience dominated by women than men. The women are much more attentive and reactive. They inspire speakers with their enthusiasm. I was told that the male audience at most of my talks is more numerous than for many other garden speakers, though I am aware that most have been persuaded to come thinking I will be talking about football. I am sure their gridiron expectations were incited by a couple of my lecture topics: Diggin' in the Dirt with the Dawg! or From Field Goals to Marigolds.

I have spoken not only in Georgia but to various gardening events in most every state in the South. One of the most memorable was speaking to the Oxford Garden Club of the Magnolia State of Mississippi. It was a luncheon, and those gracious ladies were dressed to the nines—all adorned with colorful and flashy hats. It reminded me of the hats worn by the ladies at the Kentucky Derby. They were a delightful audience.

A surprise invitation to speak came in 2007 from the Bartlett Tree Research Company located in Stamford, Connecticut, on the celebration of their centennial. It again begged the question: Why in the world am I being asked to speak to such a highly regarded national and international tree company? I discovered the company has research laboratories in New Jersey, North Carolina, and England, and some hundred offices worldwide.

Despite my "why me" concerns, it turned out to be a marvelous experience learning about the "world's leading scientific tree and shrub care company" and touring the magnificent 350-acre arboretum and research facility outside of Charlotte, the site of the celebration. My guide on that celebration day touring the arboretum was Mr. Robert A. Bartlett Jr., chairman and CEO of the company and grandson of the original founder, Dr. Francis A. Bartlett. I later found out Robert Bartlett was a Georgia graduate, which I am sure explains why I was asked to speak at the celebration. It was challenging but a great learning experience.

One of my most challenging speeches came when I was asked by Ted Plogren, a member of the Atlanta Botanical Garden, to speak to their fund-raising sponsors luncheon. I had gotten to know Ted and his lovely wife, Pat, after touring their exquisite garden in the Vinings neighborhood in Atlanta. The garden has a rustic charm about it, and I admire the fact that Pat and Ted are a real team in designing and working in this delightful garden.

Their admirable garden compatibility is in stark contrast to Barbara and me. We both have strong opinions with different tastes and modes of operation. After going around and around, we finally struck a compromise. Barbara is in charge of domestic affairs and has the final say on all things in the house. I have been assigned as chief of foreign affairs and I have the final decision on garden matters. At least she lets me think so.

THE BOTANICAL LUNCHEON

The luncheon took place in 2002 not long after Mary Pat Matheson was named the new executive director of the Atlanta Botanical Garden. This energetic lady, who has done some fabulous things in remolding and upgrading the garden, specifically wanted me to speak on the importance of supporting the Atlanta Botanical Garden. I don't like being too restricted while talking, but I thought this would be a good time for me to research the importance of supporting botanical gardens and arboretums, and particularly the Atlanta Botanical Garden.

I turned to my trusting mentor Dr. Dirr and he came through with ten reasons to support the garden, which I used as the basis of my talk. The rationale of support is so well written it is worth documenting.

1. Provides a sanctuary, an oasis, for reflection, meditation and peaceful coexistence with nature. The world moves at a dizzying pace. In the garden, time magically appears to slow down.

2. Serves as a center for like-minded people to coalesce and share their concepts and knowledge about plants, conservation, ecology, design, ad infinitum. Offers symposiums, workshops, and classes with universal appeal.

3. Acts as a repository for threatened and endangered species. Vital programs in propagation, reproductive biology, genetics, habitat preservation, etc., can be structured around the plant collections.

4. The *universal* appeal of gardening brings together all races and creeds, transcending socioeconomic status.

5. Fosters appreciation for the preservation of green spaces and their contribution to the vitality of the city.

6. Entices visitors and serves as a tourist attraction. Serves as a piece of the museum-and-attractions puzzle that broadens the education of the citizenry and out-of-city visitors. Is the green heartbeat of Atlanta.

7. Works with the parks and school system to introduce children to plants. Fostering appreciation for the green world guarantees a continuum of stewardship for the environment from future generations.

8. Assembles plants from the corners of the globe for education, preservation, and research. Displays the newest plant introductions that offer promise for Atlanta gardens.

9. Commingles horticulture, botany, art, and design into an understandable whole. Synergistically, the whole becomes greater than the parts. Art in the garden programs entice visitors who otherwise might never come. ABG has demonstrated that it thinks holistically about serving Atlanta and Georgia.

10. With its established credibility, ABG should be the purveyor of logic and data for green space creation and preservation, tree-planting initiatives, and the coalescing agent for all green groups.

The luncheon itself was a special treat; I got to sit next to Mrs. Celestia (Lessie) Smithgall, one of the most energetic and delightful people I have ever been around. I have, on a few other occasions, enjoyed the company of this ninety-eight-years-young charming former University of Georgia coed, and it was a treat to visit with her again. I remember her telling me that she had been a classmate at Georgia with the late Mrs. William (Jean) Mathis, who was so gracious and generous in allowing me to lease part of her adjacent land for an ornamental garden that today is called the Mathis garden. Since I last talked with Lessie, she has written a delightful book about her fascinating life entitled *I Took the Fork*. The title is an offshoot from one of Yogi Berra's famed Yogisms: "If you come to a fork in the road, take it!"

I was unaware but found out at the luncheon that Lessie and her husband, the late Charlie Smithgall, and the family had donated 185 acres of their homeplace in Gainesville to the Atlanta Botanical Garden for an arboretum. I have visited this wonderful woodland, a portion of which resides on Lake Lanier. Currently the botanical garden staff, under the capable direction of Mildred Pinnell Fockele, is making good use of a small part of the land as a breeding and propagation site. There are some exciting plans that, when completed, will eventually turn the entire area into an enchanting woodland garden. When the multiphase Smithgall woodland garden is complete, it will possibly be the largest of its kind in the United States. The many diverse plants planned in the garden include 150 species of deciduous magnolias and 250 species and cultivars of hydrangeas.

The last speech appearance of special significance I will mention took place at the Smith-Gilbert Arboretum during the dedication and celebration of the city of Kennesaw's purchase of a sixteen-acre, unique, private property owned and developed by Dr. Robert Gilbert and Richard Smith. The beautifully developed property provides a captivating natural landscape that is currently being renovated and upgraded for a public garden that will contribute to the education, culture, and tourism of Cobb County and the metropolitan Atlanta area.

This arboretum property features an 1840s-era plantation house, thirty pieces of outdoor sculpture, and a collection of exotic plants (some 3,000 trees, plants, and shrubs) primarily from Japan and China that attract migratory birds with over 120 different species identified.

My acting as honorary host of the celebration has taken on a significant role since this writing. I now am in a consulting role, exploring the possibility of starting a football program at Kennesaw State University, currently the fastest-growing university in Georgia with an enrollment of some 23,000. My job will require my presence in Cobb County three or four times a week, which will provide an opportunity to slow down and pause from a fast-paced consultancy and enjoy the Cobb County Kennesaw arboretum treasure.

THE GARDEN GROWS

Meanwhile, the changes over the last few years in the thirty-acre Atlanta Botanical Garden, located in the heart of the

Abies koreana, cones
Korean Fir

Abies koreana 'Horstmann's Silberlocke'
Korean Fir

city, have been astounding. In addition to the interactive children's garden and the world-renowned orchid center, an edible plant garden, a cascades garden, and fifteen acres of urban woodlands featuring a canopy walk has all just been opened. All the while the garden continues its traditional mission of education and research. Conservation had been a key focus of the garden, especially working with native pitcher plants (*Sarracenia* species), orchids, tropical conifers, and even poison dart frogs.

I was especially interested in the safeguarding initiative of the *Torreya taxifolia* (stinking cedar), an ancient species belonging to the yew family. It's referred to as the Florida *Torreya*, since its natural range is in the Florida Panhandle along the Apalachicola River, though some do exist in southwest Georgia along Lake Seminole. Today the plant is recognized as "one of North America's most critically endangered species . . . stranded in a increasingly hostile niche without any natural means of escape or survival." The Atlanta Botanical Garden has done great conservation work with the plant but admits it "faces a long road to recovery."

I toured the garden recently with Mildred Pinnell Fockele and Amanda Campbell, both superb horticulturists who incidentally are Georgia graduates. They, along with the entire botanical garden staff led by Jamie Blackburn, curator of Woodland Gardens, toured my garden as part of their annual garden tour series. When I reciprocated by touring the Atlanta Botanical Garden, we discussed the *Torreya* conservation initiative. Mildred gave me a couple of plants for my garden but warned me to be careful petting the foliage because of the sharp point of the needles. The advice was appreciated but not necessary, because I had experienced the piercing touch of the *Torreya* while earlier touring the Cox Arboretum. I have them in an out-of-the-way area of my garden away from playful grandchildren, thanks to a strong recommendation from Barbara.

As is always the case when touring a garden, I saw a must-have plant on the last Atlanta botanical walk—a Korean fir (*Abies koreana*) called 'Horstmann's Silberlocke'. It is a good-looking specimen that grabbed my immediate attention with its curled, bright silver-backed needles. Pursuing this rare conifer I am sure will lead me to the West Coast around Portland, Oregon, where the greatest majority of these cone-bearing specimens are commercially grown.

I first became aware of Callaway Gardens while a student attending Auburn University in the early 1950s. It wasn't the gardens that were the attraction at the time but rather a beach with a beautiful lake for the many Auburn students to picnic, sun, and swim.

While at Auburn I played football for the legendary Ralph "Shug" Jordan, who gave me my first opportunity in coaching when I finished my tour of duty with the Marine Corps. Coach Jordan passed away in 1980, but his lovely wife, Evelyn, who became an avid gardener, is still active at the young age of ninety-six.

I was invited to speak at Callaway Gardens several years ago, and to my amazement, sitting in the front row was Evelyn Jordan—a wonderful surprise! We had a great visit, and I have often thought, *Who would believe that in 1951 this young Auburn freshman football player would one day be lecturing on gardening to my head football coach's wife?*

I watched with special interest as Bo Callaway fulfilled and even surpassed the dreams of his parents, Cason and Virginia Callaway, the founders of the garden in the 1930s. The garden has grown since those early years to 13,000 acres and has developed into a multifaceted resort. Much credit goes to the general manager, Harold Northrop, who arrived in 1969 and for over twenty years was the driving force in taking the garden to the next level. Harold was responsible for the additions of the John A. Sibley Horticulture Center and the Cecil B. Day Butterfly Center. I developed a special interest in the garden while Harold was general manager. His son, Foster Northrop, now a vet doctor for thoroughbred racehorses in Louisville, Kentucky, played for me.

I visit the garden at least once a year and marvel at the passing of the torch from one Callaway generation to the next—each in turn taking the garden and resort to a new level. When I visit each year I am usually escorted by

Rhododendron prunifolium
Plumleaf Azalea

Callaway's publicity director, Rachel Crumbly, who worked for Barbara as a Georgia student. She always takes me to the Callaway brothers' azalea bowl, a forty-acre garden with more than 3,400 hybrid azaleas. The best time to visit is when the abundant native plumleaf azaleas (*Rhododendron prunifolium*) with their red-to-orange flowers are in bloom. They are the last native azaleas to bloom in my garden. The Callaways have adopted the plumleaf as the theme of the garden resort, and the flower design is on everything in the resort and the garden.

The Callaways also make good use of subtle signs with poetic messages placed throughout the garden. They add to the ambience and are good for the gardens. There is one at the entrance that is a favorite: "Take nothing from these gardens except: nourishment for the soul, consolation for the heart, and inspiration for the mind."

Each time I go I turn more attention to the 7.5 acres of Mr. Cason's vegetable garden, which includes vegetables, fruits, herbs, and flowers. The garden was the site of the popular PBS television show *The Victory Garden*. My next project is to expand what had been a very meager vegetable-and-herb garden into one of respectability. My vegetable garden inspiration comes from my two biggest critics: my neighbor and longtime friend Loran Smith and Barbara. Loran, a country boy who grew up on a farm in Wrightsville, Georgia, is an author, radio personality, longtime Bulldog employee, and promoter extraordinaire. His standard question whenever my name is connected with gardening is, "Why don't you grow something you can eat?" which his daddy did all his life. Barbara, who loves to cook, is constantly asking the same question. I have appeased her with a few tomato plants and herbs, but most of the time they are not productive. Next year I am taking some serious steps to a successful kitchen garden. My biggest problem now is finding enough space with sun. When I do I will start small and learn as I go.

I picked out a good model featured in the special section of the March 2009 issue of *Southern Living* and I am going to start with a rectangular raised bed and go from there. I have all the details outlined by the author, Rebecca Bull Reed. She starts the article with, "Anyone who loves to eat [that'd be me] . . . and has an interest in cooking [that'd be Barbara] should plant a kitchen garden." As soon as I finish this book, that is my next project.

Aquilegia
Columbine

A HIDDEN SECRET

The best hidden secret, not only in Georgia but in the entire Southeast and beyond, is a 300-acre soon-to-open public garden and manor house in Cherokee County just north of Atlanta. The 260-acre portion of this garden is named for Jim Gibbs, founder of a highly successful family-owned-and-operated landscape business in Atlanta. Gibbs has in recent years passed the business torch to his son David and son-in-law Peter Copses in order to devote himself full time to the development of the garden, a passion that many times becomes an incredible disease, of which I am familiar.

Not only is Jim an excellent landscaper but he knows and loves plants, and that combination of design and installation has enabled his company to be ultrasuccessful. Like all good plantsmen, he likes to share. He gave me a *Hydrangea arborescens* 'Grandiflora' (Hills of Snow), a favorite of his. Jim likes the small snowball flowers because they do not weigh the stems down. I have it planted next to the pool, and it has performed well. He also sent me seeds from his blue and purple columbine (*Aquilegia*) that he acquired from the garden of the impressionist painter Claude Monet in Giverny. He sent along some helpful planting tips, such as mixing the seed with wet sand for better distribution. I have them sowed in three separate beds and am looking forward to having Monet making a columbine appearance in my garden this spring.

Barbara accompanied me on the Gibbs garden tour that was arranged by our longtime friends Ken and Billie Rice. Ken was an All-American football player at Auburn while I was coach there, and Billie was a math teacher working on her master's. They live in Big Canoe and are good friends of Jim and Sally Gibbs. Ken, very successful in the contracting business, constructed all of the many bridges that Jim had built in the bog area of the garden. When we completed the tour and later had dinner that night with the Gibbses and Rices, Barbara's comment about the tour was, "It doesn't get any better than that." I agreed, especially since we started the tour that day with a history of the property, a basic priority of mine.

The Gibbs purchased the property in July 1980, and Jim and Sally completed the elegant manor house and surrounding forty-acre garden known as Arbor Crest in 1987. The house, located on the highest crest of the property, has a magnificent view of some of north Georgia's most beautiful mountaintops. Since 1987 Gibbs has patiently developed the remaining 260 acres into a magnificent garden for all seasons. From the manor house flow eleven long, winding trails with a concentration of garden treats of rhododendrons, hydrangeas, Japanese maples, and daylilies. Without realizing it, the path slowly leads you downward 145 feet to the crown jewel of the entire complex—a stunning Japanese garden. It is the most complete and finest oriental garden I have ever seen.

THE "PLEASANTS"

Before traversing the Japanese garden, special note should be made of the bog garden that occupies the low area. Next to the Japanese garden are a series of plain benches in the area where people can pause in the "Pleasants"—a place history describes as a "shady rest area." We paused briefly in the Pleasants and watched the wonders of the bogs before proceeding to the Japanese garden.

In Japanese culture, garden making is a high art, and Jim, using a variety of garden elements, has stayed true to the theme that everything in a Japanese garden is symbolic. There are a series of ponds and streams and waterfalls, all fulfilling the Japanese reverence for water as a source of purification. To connect the numerous ponds, a series of bridges have been tastefully built, including an exact replica of the famous arch bridge in Monet's Garden in Giverny. There is also a three-zigzag bridge, customarily used daily

in Japanese gardens to ward (or zag) off the evil spirits that follow one each day.

Stones—large and small—are a major component of Japanese gardens. Jim has patiently utilized his artistic and aesthetic design talents in this vital element of a Japanese garden. With time and extensive research, he has found in the wild, and then aesthetically and precisely placed, a series of rocks, each fulfilling a spiritual component of his Japanese garden. He can expound on each one, from the mountain rock to the prayer rock. Lanterns are occasionally placed with the stones along the water paths.

Jim has made tasteful use of varied and aristocratic Japanese maples, especially several cascading over the ponds. Through training and pruning, the garden is dotted with twisted and bent pines and other conifers to portray the image of the ancient survival of the elderly and a salute to their passing the test of time. There are cherries, maples, water lilies, and lotus all adding to the palette of the garden and seasonal color. Jim is especially proud of the wide color combination and the way the reflection on the water highlights the plants throughout the garden.

I would be remiss if I did not mention Gibbs's children's sculpture garden consisting of a variety of bronzes, each depicting the various personalities of Sally and Jim's seven grandchildren. Barbara fell in love with it and wanted to do the same for our grandchildren, but Sally and Jim's "seven" is a better financial bargain than our "eleven"!

The entire garden is truly a *shiki no sona*, or "a four seasons garden," as Gibbs proudly proclaims. I noticed, however, as we toured the garden that Gibbs was constantly referring to a different area where there are future plans. It reminded me of the axiom that gardens are never finished, and Gibbs's garden has been a work in progress for over ten years. I wondered when, if ever, it will be finished. At least—in my lifetime. It is an unfinished masterpiece that needs to be seen and shared by the world.

CHAPTER SEVEN

THE
HORTICULTURE
WORLD

COMRADES, COMPETITORS, AND CHARACTERS

One of the most rewarding experiences of my horticulture journey has been to get to know people in the industry, mostly in the
Southeast, who became an integral part of my fascinating journey.
All are down-to-earth people who share a common love for the soil and a
passion for plants and trees.

I heard one nurseryman say, "Your best friend might be your greatest
competitor," and there is a lot of truth to that statement. It is somewhat
akin to a New Zealand Kiwi—not the plant but the sheep farmers from
those down-under islands. Several years ago Barbara and I stayed a few
nights with a New Zealand couple on a sheep farm. There are many hundreds of farms on the islands, with millions of sheep. Our host and hostess were a delightful couple; the husband tending to the sheep duties. His
best friend and competitor had a farm close by and had a sheep crisis
while we were there, so our host immediately left and spent the day with
his competitor friend to help solve his problem, while neglecting his own
farm. I recall his wife remorsefully saying, "That is typical of these Kiwis.
They just go along in life helping others and not caring about their own
welfare!" While some of the nursery people I've met have some Kiwi in

them, others prescribe to the competitive American way, especially when it comes to the discovery of new plants. They are guarded with their special collections and unwilling to share until the plant potential is realized and a legal patent has been established on their find.

Their attitude about me has been quite the contrary. They feel no competitive threat and most appreciate my horticulture interest, which they feel is good for the industry. They know that I garden for pleasure and not for profit. They have been willing to share, enabling me to secure a wide variety of some of the newest and best plants before they even come on the market. That explains why my little plant kingdom has often been called a "mini botanical garden."

There are some really outstanding nursery people in the business. Some grow a wide variety of plants while others specialize in one or more varieties like camellia, hydrangeas, Japanese maples, and native azaleas. They all garden for pleasure but they also garden for profit.

It would be most difficult to name all of the fine people I have met, though I will from time to time refer to some. I would be remiss, however, not to talk about four of the most respected nursery people I have had the privilege of knowing in the industry. Don Shadow, the late Tommy Dodd Jr., Eddie Aldridge, and Hulyn Smith are highly regarded by their peers for their leadership and professionalism.

However, before expounding on these distinguished gentlemen, I would be further remiss if I didn't at least mention Felder Rushing of Jackson, Mississippi, and Ryan Gainey of Decatur, Georgia. They are the most unusual horticulture characters I have ever met.

A few years ago I was on a show with Felder Rushing in Mobile called *Festival of Flowers*. He drove up in an old pickup with a flower bed, in full bloom, in the back of his truck. For over an hour he kept everybody entertained with his "work hard at relaxing and having as much fun as possible—with as little effort as practical" philosophy.

There is no way to describe his exotic and outrageous way of gardening, which matches his earthy looks and personality. You would have to see him and his garden to believe it, and the best way to do that is through his Web site, felderrushing.net. Despite it all, this unique character is a seventh-generation Mississippi gardener, author, columnist, and host of radio and gardening programs.

Another interesting character is Ryan Gainey, a talented landscape designer with a unique private garden. Ryan gave me a tour of his garden, which has been appropriately described as a "garden of poetry and prose!" It is full of interesting "rooms" and architectural delights. I was intrigued, for instance, with the diminutive temples Ryan designed overlooking the koi pond. There is a *Hydrangea arborescens* ('Ryan Gainey'; I am proud to have one in my garden), and he uses his namesake to salute a statue of "winter" inserted in an architectural niche. These and many more treats make up this eccentric garden. Ryan says the garden is "the story of my life."

According to Ryan, his life story started with "those childhood memories and the distinct smell of the lovely flowers" in the fall, especially colorful chrysanthemums (mums). Ryan has a love of plant history and there is no plant with a more interesting history than mums. Armitage calls it "one of the oldest cultivated plants in existence," dating back to 500 BC in China. Ryan recalls mums being used by the Catholic countries in Europe to honor the dead on All Souls Day, though he thinks the tribute should be a "celebration of life not death." He has taken pass-along mum plants from sharing friends and introduced to the gardening world several colorful cultivars such as 'Ryan's Pink', 'Ryan's Yellow', and the amazing orange 'Thanksgiving Day'. From the latter (to his own surprise) he produced the multicolored 'Ryan's Rainbow', destined to be one of the most popular chrysanthemums of the future.

The novel colors of 'Ryan's Rainbow' will match some

of the eccentric formal attire I have seen him wear on occasions. Some of his colorful outfits would rival the attire of some of the great maharajas of India.

Gardening embraces all people, and Ryan Gainey and Felder Rushing are great examples of the distinctive characters who have given much to the gardening world.

DON SHADOW

Nurseryman extraordinaire Don Shadow is known around the world as one of the most active acquirers of unusual plants. His grandfather moved from Warsaw, Indiana, to Winchester, Tennessee, in 1872 to grow fruit. I asked Shadow why, and he expounded on the fact that the area had many Confederate sympathizers during the Civil War, and his grandfather, being one of them, wanted to work and raise his family in the South. I learned that southern and middle Indiana was initially settled by southerners, and those early settlers had economic ties to the South. I also learned that in February 1861, Shelby County, southeast of Indianapolis, even voted to secede from Indiana after the state barely voted to join the Union. Many wanted to let the South go in peace. Ironically Franklin County, where Shadow's nursery is located, seceded from Tennessee in February 1861 when the state did not initially secede from the Union along with other Deep South states. The county even petitioned Confederate Alabama to annex it, but the issue became moot after Tennessee eventually seceded.

Don Shadow's grandfather was at home in the South in the fruit business, raising his nine boys. Shadow's father continued in the nursery business and sent young Don off to the University of Tennessee for a formal education in horticulture. This young Tennessee boy was first housed in a crowded room in Neyland Football Stadium, and he told his dad the four walls were closing in on him, and he was coming home to be outside again on the farm. His dad

Vince Dooley and Don Shadow

found him a small room between the university greenhouses with an outside bathroom, which was no bother to him. Don was happy, earned his degree in horticulture, and returned home to the nursery business. Shadow said living in the greenhouses for four years enabled him to get cuttings of some of the newest introductions, and by the time he graduated he was way ahead of the game.

I have had the privilege of visiting the Shadow Nursery on several occasions, and each extended visit was like I had been there for the first time. I never cease to be amazed at the variety of plant and tree finds Don has brought back to his nursery either from the Tennessee fields or from Japan, where he embarks with a few friends on an annual visit. As you would imagine, all of those who make the trip to the Far East are just as passionate as Shadow in finding and introducing new plants.

I would be remiss if I didn't mention one of those who makes the annual trip to Japan with Don Shadow. Ted Stephens of Nurseries Caroliniana in North Augusta, South Carolina, is a quiet giant in the industry. However, he gets worked up showing the gems of his private collection from his trips to Japan. He is also very kindhearted and has shared some of his introductions with me.

Halesia diptera var. magniflora
Two-wing Silverbell

One of the most interesting introductions by Ted is the original Asian wisteria, *Wisteria sinensis*, that was introduced by the Berckmann family, who acquired Fruitland Nurseries in the early 1800s. The plant is still growing at the Augusta National golf course and can often be seen in flower during the Masters. Stephens, whose family helped save the plant, noticed that the flower had a wonderful fragrance and, amazingly, flowered in a gallon container. Consequently, cuttings from the original tree, labeled 'Augusta Pride', became a popular nursery item. I have one near the pool and patio area where I can control this runaway prize. Each spring it puts on a spectacular flower show, pleasing to the sight and smell. However, I do have to prune it once a week throughout the spring and summer.

It is on my bucket list to one day go with Ted, Don, and another obsessed plantsman, Ozzie Johnson, to Japan and meet some of the great nursery people of that country. Ozzie is with Saul's Nursery and makes the trip every year. He is probably more connected in Japan than all the other passionate journeymen because his late wife, Jitsuko, was from that country and they traveled often together to her homeland. Ozzie is regarded as one of the top plantsmen in the Southeast who has enriched every

aspect of horticulture in that region.

While I was visiting Ozzie's garden a few years ago, he told me about a Japanese maple that he described as the "weeper of all weepers." He found the maple in Japan, brought it back, and named it 'Ryusen'. He told me it was going to be introduced into the market through Saul's Nursery and gave me a tiny one about a foot high. These green weepers bow straight to the ground and must be staked to get some height. Ozzie's gift is now about head high, comes straight down, and spreads out as it hits the ground. Ozzie's comrades, the Saul brothers, Bobby and Richard, great nurserymen and supportive friends, later gave me a taller-than-me 'Ryusen' that attracts the immediate attention of people touring the garden.

Ozzie and the Saul family formalized a close relationship in 1998 by cofounding ItSaul Nursery. The partnership led to a special relationship with Lisa Bartlett, a nursery manager of the company. They have been together for almost a decade with the promise of many more to come as evidenced by his answer to my "What next?" question. Ozzie said, with a grin, "To spend quality time in the garden, a glass of wine, good food, and Lisa by my side."

Ozzie will always be in the pursuit of new plants in the Far East, and while I have that desire to go to Japan with him, I have no desire to join his fever-struck buddies traveling to other places in Asia. Each year Ozzie and his friends—Scott McMahan, whose nursery is in Clermont, Georgia, and Dan Hinkley, who once owned Heronswood Nursery in Kingston, Washington—travel to various Asian countries in search of new plants. They have taken backpacking safaris to China, Korea, Vietnam, and Taiwan, and they have brought back an extraordinary number of plants. Despite my newly acquired plant passion, these guys have ascended (literally climbing some mountains from five to ten thousand feet) to a level of total obsession. Meanwhile, I will continue my relatively modest journey, learning from the more-matured, still-obsessed Don Shadow and Ted Stephens.

THE SHADOW NURSERY

The best way to appreciate the esteem in which Shadow and Stephens are held by their peers is to visit a trade show and watch their booth. It is always crowded with admiring nursery people anxious to learn of the newest introductions. You can bet it will be a plant with variegation or weeping qualities.

Shadow has often been accused of holding them so that only in the confines of Shadow Nursery does a particular specimen exist. They point to a two-wing silver bell (*Halesia diptera* var. *magniflora*) loaded with large white flowers from the top to the bottom of the tree that he had for eighteen years before giving it the name 'Southern Snow'. Then there is a fourteen-foot, gold-leaf, trident maple that he has yet to name.

I went with Dirr on my third trip to the Shadow nursery. I immediately became infatuated with a hybrid dogwood *Cornus* 'Celestial Shadow'. The leaves are variegated with yellow margins, and the flowers, as Shadow says, "look you squarely in the eye!" When we were leaving he gave me several plants and asked if there was anything in particular I wanted, and I mentioned the 'Celestial Shadow' dogwood, not knowing he had not released the plant and had them only at the nursery. I was embarrassed when be brought me one, saying, "This is the first one that has left the Shadow Nursery." I have it potted and securely placed in the patio and guard it with extraordinary care.

Meanwhile, Dirr had heart palpitations when he saw a golden-leaf tulip poplar (*Liriodendron tulipifera* 'Tennessee Gold'). I took a few great pictures of these two masters by the tree discussing its merits.

It was a treat to ride around the nursery in the backseat

Cornus florida × *C. kousa* 'Celestial Shadow'
Dogwood Hybrid

for a full day quietly listening to them discuss plants and trees. Later we spent some quality time with our good friend Fred Hooks, who has formed a partnership with Shadow. Hooks runs a division called All Things Acer, specializing in Japanese maples and boasting over 400 varieties. Hooks is an amazing Japanese maple man, and he has shared several with me, including some of his newest introductions.

Before he embarked on his dream job with his beloved Japanese maples, Fred was the ultrasuccessful president of Post Landscape Properties. His work with Post Properties and later with his own company set the bar for landscape design and selective plant installation for high-end rental apartments from south Florida to northern Virginia. His use of mass color in the spring coupled with selective specimen plants as the base elevated simple apartment living to a spectacular resort-site setting.

The unique partnership of All Things Acer between Don Shadow and Fred Hooks will be interesting to watch. Fred will be running the Japanese maple part of the company while Don will be multitasking with all of his plants and animals.

No visit to the Shadow Farm is complete without seeing some of his rare animals, most of which are threatening

Cercis canadensis 'Hearts of Gold'
Redbud

Nyssa sylvatica 'Sheri's Cloud'
Tupelo

to become extinct worldwide. Since many of the zoos are not breeding some of these rare animals, Shadow is determined to keep them going and is constantly hauling rare specimens from zoos around the world. His passion for breeding these rare specimens has and will keep many species from becoming extinct.

How Shadow keeps up with it all is beyond me. For sure one answer is his wife, Mary, a most gracious lady, who somehow tolerates his energy and passion. Then there is their daughter, Jennifer, who has taken on more and more responsibility with the nursery. Jennifer has given a special gift to her parents: three sons who are the apples of their eyes. Elijah, little Evan, and Ethan are often seen riding around with Pop Pop, learning the nursery trade and life on the farm from their Tennessee farm grandfather.

Dirr and I wanted to visit a couple of other nurseries in the area, but since time always runs out, we found ourselves in a near impossible situation until Don took charge. He arranged for us to visit two other nurseries in Franklin County before heading back to meet a deadline in Athens.

At the last Georgia Green Industry show, I visited with Ray and Cindy Jackson and was excited about their new find, an upright gold-leaf redbud (*Cercis canadensis*) called 'The Rising Sun'. They wanted me to have one to spread the word, so I was anxious to add this new one to my redbud collection. Thanks to the Jacksons' generosity I have it planted in the pool area under an Asian fringe tree (*Chionanthus retusus*). The Jacksons have a great collection of Japanese maples and dogwoods.

Afterward we had lunch with Harald Neubauer and his son Alex of Hidden Hollow Nursery. Harald came from Germany and worked for Don Shadow before starting his own nursery. He had visited my garden earlier, and Barbara and I both thought he was a pleasant gentleman. Dirr and I spent an exciting hour in the father-son special collection greenhouse. Generosity prevailed once again, and I picked up a variegated black tupelo (*Nyssa sylvatica* 'Sheri's Cloud') and a 'Lemon-Lime' leaf witch hazel (*Hamamelis virginiana*). Dirr and I left with great anticipation of a new purple leaf redbud weeper (*Cercis canadensis* 'Ruby Falls'). The plant was named by Harald's grandson (Alex's boy) who liked the "Visit Ruby Falls" highway signs he always noticed while riding in the car. I enjoy the history of plant naming and the 'Ruby Falls' redbud is a great one. This unique redbud was bred by Dr. Dennis Werner of North Carolina State University.

The beloved Tom Dodd, born in 1915 in Mobile, Alabama, was called by Eddie Aldridge the "finest man I have ever known, an angel on earth!" Those sentiments speak to the high esteem and respect in which Mr. Dodd was held in the horticulture industry. Sadly, while writing the initial draft on Mr. Dodd, I learned that he passed away on May 7, 2009, at the age of ninety-four. I have kept the initial bio of Mr. Dodd, adjusting the text and elaborating where appropriate.

Tom's father was in the nursery business and was known as a superior propagator. He loved it so much he let other family members run the business while he was in the greenhouses.

Tom Jr. inherited his father's propagating ability and passed it on to his son, Tommy, who now runs the Dodd and Dodd business. Prior to Mr. Dodd's death, young Tom Jr. ran the business under the watchful eye of his father. At ninety-four Mr. Dodd seldom failed to come to the nursery, usually in the morning, advising and propagating.

When I would visit Mobile I always tried to spend a little time with Mr. Dodd and his spry wife, Elizabeth, the true family matriarch. Invariably Mr. Dodd would take me out to his home garden, pointing out the plants, the history, and the parents. While speaking to Mrs. Dodd after her husband's passing, she was happy I had come by to visit about a month before he died.

Mr. Dodd has introduced a lot of plants, but the most noted is the "Confederate Series." He propagated the series with son Tommy, a Citadel graduate who has a keen knowledge of the "great unpleasantness," as he calls it. The plants are named after Confederate Civil War heroes. By taking the heat-tolerant Florida azalea (*Rhododendron austrinum*) and crossing it with the larger-flowered Exbury azalea 'Hotspur yellow', they have given the industry some beautiful native azaleas with pleasant fragrance.

Rhododendron 'Admiral Semmes'
Hybrid Native Azalea

They have also given me some to experiment with, especially knowing my interest in the Civil War. I love them all, the orange of 'Robert E. Lee' and many more, but my favorite is 'Admiral Semmes' with its beautiful, fragrant, yellow flowers that I have located in several places in the garden.

Mr. Dodd introduced several hollies, especially those crossed with the bigleaf *Ilex latifolia*. One of his latest introductions was a fragrant *Camellia sasanqua* named 'Miss Auburn', after his beloved alma mater. Mr. Dodd loved Auburn and traveled to Auburn for every home game, but in the last few years watched the games on TV in the hotel room while his wife, who still has that special Auburn spirit, was at the games shouting, "War Eagle!" Every time Mr. Dodd would give me a plant or send a few by Tommy, they were always ribbon-tied with the Auburn school colors, orange and blue.

While Mr. Dodd had given me some wonderful plants, he gave Auburn practically a whole campus of plants and trees. Some people estimate the value to be between two and three million dollars.

Mr. Dodd gave the greatest number of his plants to Auburn, but he also shared some plants with Auburn's

Rhododendron 'Stonewall Jackson'
Hybrid Native Azalea

great rival, Alabama, and with the Catholic Jesuit College in Mobile, Spring Hill. At the memorial service in Mobile at the Spring Hill Baptist Church, the minister recalled two humorous horticulture stories told to him by Tommy Jr. about his dad's gifts to the other schools.

When the Alabama president received the gift, he asked Mr. Dodd for special instructions for the plant. Mr. Dodd told him that since they were Auburn plants they would be more vigorous and happier if each morning he would look to the sunrise and shout, "War Eagle!" The Alabama president thanked him politely but told him he did not think it would be wise to do that.

Likewise, when the monsignor at Spring Hill College asked for advice on the plants given to the school, Mr. Dodd told him that they were Baptist plants and they needed to be fully immersed!

While Mr. Dodd was proud of sharing his plants, he was especially proud of presenting Auburn with the complete set of *Curtis Botanical Magazine*. On my last visit he wanted me to go to the Auburn library to see them. At the time I didn't know what the *Curtis Botanical* was, but I told him I would do it. I soon found out that the *Curtis Botanical* was first published in 1787 in London by

botanist and horticulturist William Curtis. The publication is now well over 200 years old and is the longest-running periodical in the world that features colored illustrations of plants. These illustrations are reproduced from watercolor originals by some of the world's leading botanical artists. I had a chance to visit the Auburn library to view a sampling of the collection in the guarded rare-book area of special collections. The books contain detailed horticulture and botanical information with references to history and the economic uses of the plant. The real value of the books are the illustrations, which are absolutely magnificent. Mr. Dodd proudly told me that there are only three complete sets of the *Curtis Botanical Magazine* in university libraries—Auburn, Cornell, and Harvard.

For all of Mr. Dodd's many contributions to Auburn, the university honored him in 1995 with an honorary doctorate. Numerous honors have been bestowed on Mr. Dodd, but the one he valued the most was his honorary doctorate from Auburn.

I had great affection for Mr. Dodd for many reasons, but the Auburn and Mobile connection made it extraordinary. I grew up in the Port City, so it is special to get to know the great history and heritage Mobile County has for horticulture. There are numerous well-respected nurseries within a five-mile radius of Mr. Dodd's house in Semmes, Alabama. Most are second- and third-generation horticulturists.

One of the first Mobile nurseries I visited after returning to my hometown after being horticulturally infected was Mr. K. Sawada. Mr. Sawada came from Japan with his father to start the nursery and became a highly respected citizen of the community. He was happy to see me, since he followed me in sports in high school in Mobile and then into college at Auburn. He gave me one of the plants he hybridized, K. Sawada, a fast-growing, early-blooming, white, formal double camellia that is still in the garden doing great. His two sons run the business now, though as

Alabama graduates they set out to get away from the nursery business but eventually came back home.

Maarten van de Giessen and his wife, Colleen, are good friends. He loves azaleas, inheriting a lot of Dr. Aromi hybrids, and has developed some great cultivars. Their good friends, Bobby and Deborah Green, from Fairhope have become good friends with Barbara and me. Bobby Green told me that Mr. Dodd was an inspiration to him as a young nurseryman.

Close by Mr. Dodd's nursery is Joe Kinney, his wife, Cherry, and son, Chad, who run the family Kinney Nursery. Joe is originally from Georgia, and we have visited on several occasions at his booth at the Green Industry show in Athens. He is always in a shirt and tie, and his booth is immaculate. His nursery was the same way when I visited a few years ago. He wanted me to try out a few plants, including two pink-flowered Titi (*Cliftonia monophylla*), which are doing great in the garden.

Bobby Green has a wonderful nursery in Fairhope, across the bay, specializing in camellias. I was last with Bobby when we met in the Red Hills of South Alabama between Camden and Monroeville (of *To Kill a Mockingbird* fame), near the Alabama River, to view the distinctive Red Hill, or May Pink, azaleas (*Rhododendron colemanii*). Joining us was Ron Miller from Pensacola, an azalea enthusiast who long has been a spokesperson for the uniqueness of the species. Also joining us was Bill Finch, Alabama environmentalist and garden writer for the *Mobile Press*. Finch also is an advocate of the newfound azalea discovered along the upper coastal plains of Alabama to the Georgia border. I had been with Bill earlier, exploring the fascinating Splinter Hill bog area northeast of Mobile. Splinter Hill is owned by the state and operated by the Nature Conservancy of Alabama. The bog area contains twelve species of carnivorous plants, including five species of pitcher plants, two of which are the rare white-topped and purple pitcher plants.

Cliftonia monophylla
Pink-flowered Titi

Several characteristics of the Red Hill azalea support its uniqueness. It is larger than most all native azaleas. We saw a gorgeous pink in the vast colony twenty feet tall, from which we took cuttings. The Red Hill blooms late, which easily separates it from similar native azaleas. Some believe it has the strongest scent of all the azaleas. For sure this colony was rich with a sweet aroma.

As we maneuvered our way through the thickest of the azalea jungle, I was surprised by the beautiful mountain laurel jungle in full bloom intermixed with the azaleas. I was more surprised to see Spanish moss that far away from the seacoast. The Red Hills are an interesting study of trees and plants. However, the Red Hill azaleas are the main attraction. As with any new species, these azaleas will undergo careful scientific scrutiny. Miller believes it will pass the test because genetic information is in the Red Hill's favor. Most of the azaleas in the world, as well as all others in the Red Hills, have two sets of chromosomes and are therefore called diploids. Tests show the Red Hill azaleas as tetraploids with twice the number of chromosomes, and thus unlikely to hybridize with the diploid azaleas in the area.

I am sure the late S.D. Coleman Jr., who found the

azalea in the 1950s and sold it out of a nursery for many years as 'May Pink' (two out of three are white), would be surprised at the commotion his find has caused. The Coleman family no doubt is proud that Mr. Coleman has been honored with the botanical name.

I first learned of *Rhododendron colemanii* from Ernest Koone while visiting his Lazy K Nursery in Pine Mountain, Georgia. Koone, a noted grower of native azaleas, wanted me to have one pink and two whites to see the color range and to see how they would do in Athens. They are doing great in my garden.

My journey to the lower part of my native state, and many journeys to my hometown of Mobile, always included a horticulture visit to my friend, the late and beloved Tom Dodd and his wife. My journeys to the south of my adopted state, Georgia, will always include a visit to the beloved Hulyn Smith, a lover of camellias and the Georgia Bulldogs.

HULYN SMITH: THE SOUTHERN CAMELLIA WORLD

If you ask any of the camellia experts who is one of the most respected camellia men, most would say Hulyn Smith of Valdosta, Georgia. No one has been more deeply involved in the American Camellia Society, located in Fort Valley, Georgia, than this Southern gentleman.

He has served as president of the society that boasts a membership of 3,000 camellia enthusiasts across the country. He has also served as chair of the research advisory committee of the society, as well as a two-time vice president for the Atlantic Coast territory and two-time chair of the board of directors. He is also known as the chief judge of camellia shows and is highly respected for the tight ship he runs in that capacity. Smith is an avid follower of the Georgia Bulldogs, and I became acquainted with him through the generosity of a few other camellia Bulldogs.

Camellia 'Christmas Candles', expanding flower buds

The late Dr. Dan Nathan, of Fort Valley, Georgia, was one of the nicest persons I have ever known. He was the epitome of the greatest generation and a longtime friend and supporter. He was a highly respected camellia man as a hybridizer and servant of the national society. Another highly respected camellia man who loved the Bulldogs was Dr. Buddy English of Warner Robins, Georgia, who inherited many of the unnamed hybrids of the highly respected hybridizer Dr. Walter Homeyer. Because of my camellia curiosity and service to the Bulldogs, Dr. Buddy and Dr. Dan wanted to name a camellia after me. They selected one of Dr. Homeyer's plants that had won two "best seedling" awards.

The camellia has large, bright, single Georgia red flowers. The anthers and the stamens are pink, and the leaves are large and dark green. The parents are three-quarter *C. japonica* for hardiness and one quarter *C. reticulata* for the large leaf and flower. The male parent is 'Red Crystal', a *C. reticulata*, and the female parent is 'Silver Lace', a *C. japonica*. Drs. Nathan and English submitted the formal application, which was accepted. The plant was registered as the 'Vince Dooley' camellia.

After the plant was registered and a few scions (cuttings) were taken, Dr. English gave the camellia to me, and it's been thriving at the entrance of the Mathis garden. There it stood for three years with no plan for propagation and distribution until I heard from Dennis Dooley, president of the Oregon Camellia Society in Scappoose, Oregon, who wanted to secure a 'Vince Dooley' camellia. This prompted me to inquire into propagating the plant, which resulted in taking several scions and sending them to several camellia hybridizer friends. It all started with Hulyn Smith. I traveled to Valdosta for a book signing, and he sat and visited for a good while during the signing. We talked Bulldogs football and camellias. I told him about next year's gridiron outlook, and he told me that Valdosta is situated in the middle of the finest growing area for camellias in the world—from my hometown, Mobile, Alabama, to Charleston, South Carolina.

Earlier in the day I had visited with Mark Crawford at his Loch Laurel Nursery in Valdosta, Georgia, who has a wide variety of camellia species. I was eager to expand my already extensive camellia collection. I didn't realize how carried away I got in securing camellias until I was asked by a journalist who was doing a story for the American Camellia Society's quarterly publication how many camellias I have. I told him I had no idea but would let him know. To my amazement I had over 120 different cultivars of the traditional *C. japonica, C. sasanqua,* and hybrid species, plus some forty more duplications. All of them are hardy for the Athens USDA zone 7.

My first acquisition of camellias came after learning that the highly regarded camellia grower Mr. George G. Gerbing Sr. of Binkley, Georgia, was going out of business and selling his stock. I made the trip to Binkley, in southeast Georgia. Mr. Gerbing and his sons dug the camellias and loaded them for my trip back to Athens. I still have them in my garden—such names as 'China Doll', 'Annita Triumph', 'Ack-Scent' (fragrant), 'Empress Variegated', and 'David Gerbing' (a son). While father and sons were digging, I was

Camellia japonica 'Scentsation'

treated to the wonderful hospitality of Mr. Gerbing's wife, Louise, a remarkable lady, who was his soul mate for fifty-nine years before he passed away in 2007.

Mrs. Gerbing sent me a copy of her father-in-law's (G. G. Gerbing) book entitled *Camellias* published in 1945. It was the first book published in America with full color pictures of camellias. G. G. Gerbing had a camellia and azalea nursery in Amelia Island, Florida, in the 1930s with over 250,000 plants of the two genera. He introduced 'G. G. Gerbing', in honor of his wife, a white-flowering sport of the *Rhododendron indica* 'George Taber'. It is still in the trade today, and I have one in my garden that was given to me by the Gerbing family.

Since my first introduction to camellias I have learned there are over 20,000 registered camellia cultivars. What is even more astonishing is that there are over 250 species in existence. It was the learning pursuit of a camellia species called *C. handelii* that drove me to Mark Crawford and his Lock Laurel Nursery. I had seen the camellia *C. handelii* with its small leaves, small white flowers, and somewhat weeping characteristics in Ted Stephens's booth at the Georgia trade show. It certainly didn't resemble the traditional camellias, so I wanted one. Not only did I pick up a

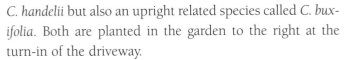
Camellia reticulata 'Clifford Parks'

Camellia 'El Dorado'

C. handelii but also an upright related species called *C. buxifolia*. Both are planted in the garden to the right at the turn-in of the driveway.

In conversing with Crawford I discovered that he had a plant biology background and was growing camellias differently in search of a way to prevent die-back on year-old plants. He grew the young plants with "capillary irrigation," which provides water without touching the foliage, thereby reducing the spread of die-back fungus. It was a little too scientific for me, but I enjoyed learning about this and his other innovative techniques—like growing camellias under a red shade cloth that changes the quality of light on young camellias and improves growth and branching.

Crawford considers Hulyn Smith "at the top" of the national camellia community and a "mentor to his own success with camellias." Smith has mutual respect for Crawford and the highest regard for his scientific knowledge.

When I got home from Valdosta, I got a call from Smith asking me to send him some scions of the 'Vince Dooley' camellia so that he and Crawford could graft some. I was pleased because not only did I want to make one available for cousin Dooley in Oregon but also there was a need to secure one for the statue garden that recently was dedicat-

ed in my honor in UGA's south campus athletic complex. Smith had to walk me through taking and mailing scions. I enjoyed the learning process; in fact, I got so confident in the technique that I started sending some to my other camellia friends and even grafted one myself under the guidance of my friend Bobby Green of Fairhope, Alabama.

Both Mark Crawford and Hulyn Smith invited me to attend their annual Valdosta Camellia Show, which they proudly call "the best in the Southeast." I took up their offer and stayed in the home of Smith's daughter, Mandy White, and her lovely family. The experience of getting to know the Smith family, especially Hulyn's wife, the vivacious Janet Smith, was a treat.

Mark and Hulyn gave me a tour of the delightful camellia show, highlighting the winners of various categories. The judges had to make some tough choices, but my overall favorite was Smith's *Camellia japonica* hybrid 'Lauren Tudor', named for his youngest daughter. This spectacular white flower with pink flecks and stripes is very large (six and a half inches in diameter), with a peony form, and was prominently displayed at the judges' reception the night before. Daughter Mandy agreed and rewarded me with one of her dad's 'Lauren Tudor' plant that I

Camellia sasanqua 'Yuletide'

have proudly displayed in the garden.

While attending the show I learned of a freak flood that hit Valdosta in April 2009 and dumped nine inches of rain in forty-eight hours, flooding the Smiths' house and covering Hulyn's prize camellias with eight feet of water for four days! With the help of Mark Crawford, who launched a relief fund, the Smiths were back in their home in four months, and miraculously 95 percent of some 400 camellias were saved. The way the camellia community rallied was a touching testimony to the high esteem in which Hulyn Smith is held.

While Smith is looked upon as the guru granddaddy among camellia people, there are several other extraordinary camellia experts.

BOBBY GREEN: CAMELLIA HISTORIAN

It has been a genuine pleasure getting to know Bobby Green and his wife, Debbie. Barbara and I have had many enjoyable evenings together with them. I always enjoy visiting Bobby's nursery in Fairhope, across the bay from Mobile where I spent some memorable summers growing up.

Bobby was one of the first camellia nurserymen that I

met, and I bonded with him early on. I admire him not only because of his knowledge and love of camellias but also because of his deep appreciation of history. He wrote a splendid booklet entitled *Winter Garden: A Resurrection of Ancient Treasures, the Camellia.* The subtitle further states, "Through Three Hundred Years Tracing the Arrival of the Plant from the Orient to the Western World."

Bobby told of his love of old things as a youngster growing up in the nursery business with a father who loved camellias and with whom he "became incredibly linked." He lost his father in 1982, but sentimentally Bobby says he still walks through the garden with him each winter, reminiscing about him naming the different plants on their walks together. He said it makes him realize the debt he owes his father for teaching him about camellias.

The booklet is a must-have for serious camellia collectors as well as casual gardeners. It lists some of the great Japonicas in four distinct historical categories: "antiques" (pre–World War I), "historical" (World War I–1949), "heirloom" (1950–59), and "Modern" (1960–present). The booklet also sketches a brief history of camellia hybrids and sasanqua, listing some of the best of those species.

Bobby has been very generous in sharing his knowledge and plants with me. A large portion of the camellia walk in my garden is a tribute to him. On my last visit Bobby broke out some scions I sent him of the 'Vince Dooley' camellia and gave me a cleft graft lesson, using sand to hold in the moisture.

Bobby enjoys searching and evaluating antique camellias, calling the exercise "one of the most rewarding camellia ventures" he has found. He has quite a collection of some of the old camellias in the "historical" category. Most were proudly introduced only to have a short life span, replaced by another with a different color or slightly larger flower. This is understandable when one considers the more than 20,000 registered camellias, with more to come.

I believe most of the attention in the future will be given to the hybridization of more and better fragrant camellias. One of the best that Bobby gave me in this category is one called 'High Fragrance', which has the best fragrance I've enjoyed so far.

Bobby plans to keep his quest for the antique camellias alive by preserving them in the winter garden that he has donated to the Mobile Botanical Garden, named in memory of his father. The garden is also a tribute to Bobby, reflecting his love and appreciation of the past to live on into the future.

Camellia reticulata × *C. Japonica*
'Vince Dooley'

TOMMY ALDEN

I also sent some scions to my friend and Bulldog supporter Tommy Alden of County Line Nursery in Byron, Georgia, whom I met before through Dr. Dan Nathan. During my last visit to Tommy's nursery he gave me a fitting pair of football-named camellias, 'Touchdown' and 'Kickoff', the latter a sport of the former. I have them close together in my garden since a 'Kickoff' always follows a 'Touchdown'.

Tommy is not only a top camellia man but the most respected grower of the winter daphne (*Daphne odora*) that fills the air with wonderful fragrant blooms in February. Every gardener experiences moments of humility, and my most humbling experience as a gardener is tied to the winter daphne.

I loved the fragrance of the plant, and when I was in my early gardening craze, I planted several under a dogwood tree located in the patio that I would enjoy each morning in the winter months on my way to the exercise room in our pool house. Several people had told me they are finicky and hard to grow because they don't like wet feet. I assumed the daphne problem was for other less-accomplished gardeners, for mine were thriving. And besides, I had just received my Master Gardner

diploma. Before long, my dogwood, that was about on its last leg after forty years, died and had to be removed. Within two months, all five of my daphnes also were gone! I was sick, but I later learned that the dogwood was taking good care of the daphnes, not only providing adequate shade but absorbing all the moisture, thus keeping their feet dry. It was a humbling experience but a good lesson. All of my new daphnes are planted high and away from moist soil and in shade to part shade. They are thriving and producing great winter fragrance, and my gardening confidence is restored.

What initially motivated me to visit Tommy that day was, of all people, an old college classmate and basketball teammate, Bill Fickling of nearby Macon, Georgia. Bill and his lovely wife, Neva Jane, Miss America 1953, and Barbara and I have kept in touch over the years.

On my last visit to Macon, I stayed with the Ficklings, and Bill gave me a tour of his garden. I was impressed with the garden's unique design, with the main path eventually leading to a prominent focal point—a life-size statue of Bill's great-grandfather who fought in the Civil War. Interestingly the statue was carved from a photograph, and when it was completed, the face looked exactly like Bill

and Neva's son, Roy. At first I thought it was a little strange to have a Confederate soldier as the focal point of a garden, but upon reflection, knowing Bill as I did in college, the garden design was vintage Bill.

Beside the unique design, Bill had some good-looking plants. During the tour I found my old teammate to be quite horticulturally knowledgeable. He is probably the only former teammate that I know that has caught plant fever like myself.

I was especially impressed with two camellias he had in his garden that I did not—'Frank Houser' and 'Frank Houser' variegated, both *Camellia reticulata*. After researching the plants I found they were introduced over twenty years ago by the late and highly respected hybridizer Dr. Walter Homeyer (he also hybridized the 'Vince Dooley' camellia) from Macon, Georgia. They are magnificent camellias, both vigorous growers with open, upright habits producing very large peony to semidouble flowers. 'Frank Houser' is red, while 'Frank Houser' variegated is rose-red with contrasting white blotches. Bradford King, writing for the American Camellia Society said that both "have almost completely dominated the ACS Camellia Hall of Fame [most best-in-show and court-honor awards]." He calls the two "the best and most popular *Camellia reticulata* of the decade." They were definitely must-have plants for my garden. Immediately after I left Bill I headed straight to Tommy Alden's place, picked up both, and now enjoy them in my garden.

I need to get Bill and Neva (Miss America still looks fantastic) to visit and tour my garden. Bill, a Kappa Alpha fraternity alumni with deep affections for the old South, will especially enjoy seeing my Confederate Rose (*Hibiscus chinensis* 'Mutablis'), Confederate jasmine (*Trachelospermum jasminoides*), and "Confederate Series" of native azalea hybrids (*Rhododendron* 'Exbury hybrids' × *R. austrinum*).

THE CAMELLIA AZALEA

As part of my search of some 'Vince Dooley' camellias I contacted Stephen Jones, a writer and photographer formerly with the American Camellia Society. Jones had written an article about my camellia interest. When he called me about the article, entitled "Hall of Fame: Football and Flowers," the recurring question came alive again: "What in the world am I doing here?" In a national camellia journal? Nevertheless, Jones, who had good knowledge of camellia experts, suggested Gene Phillips of Savannah, a nurseryman highly regarded in the camellia world and a strong advocate of the Southeastern Camellia Society headquartered in the Georgia port city.

I arranged to meet Gene on a Savannah trip at the famous Coastal Plains Bamboo Garden and to bring him some scions that he wanted to graft. He later asked for some cuttings, so I sent him some to be rooted. On my way to Savannah, I was curious as to why Phillips wanted to meet at the state-owned bamboo garden, but I soon found out that the University of Georgia had granted the Southeast Camellia Society a couple of acres of land to the right entrance to develop a camellia species garden. The initial phase of the garden had just been planted. He gave me a tour, introducing me to some species I had never heard of. The garden has great potential and a lot more planting space. I am anxious to see it again on some of my future Savannah trips.

Before leaving, Gene introduced me to the latest camellia buzz, a summer-blooming *Camellia azalea*. He had one grafted for me that I now have in my container garden on the patio. I was warned that it was tender and needed to be brought indoors in the wintertime. It was fascinating learning about the new species from an article Gene had written in the summer 2006 issue of *Southeastern Camellia Digest*.

Phillips had read an article in the *International Camellia Journal* by a camellia expert from China, Professor Gao Jiyin, about this summer-blooming camellia species found in Guangdong Province, China, in 1986. Phillips contacted our top camellia man, Hulyn Smith, who was able to negotiate the shipment of several *Camellia azalea* cuttings, as did Longwood Gardens in Kennett Square, Pennsylvania. The experience at Longwood and with Smith representing the American Camellia Society was the same. The plant did not grow well from rooted cuttings but did respond to cleft grafting. Both Longwood and Smith, working with Mark Crawford, had plants that bloomed in the hot weather. Crawford told me that the *C. azalea* is marginal growing in Valdosta, and the best zone is 9 in Orlando, Florida. Smith encouraged Phillips to experiment in his "Gene's nursery," and he had some buds that opened in 98-degree weather. Phillips said that he has been growing camellias all of his life with various degrees of excitement, but nothing ever excited him as much as seeing a summer-blooming camellia species blooming in his garden.

To add to the excitement, hybridizing is now taking place among growers in the United States, crossing *Camellia azalea* with *Camellia amplexicaulis*. The latter is a Vietnam find that is cold-hardy and has the potential to rebloom. Crossing *Camellia amplexicaulis* with *Camellia azalea*, which also has reblooming qualities and thrives in hot weather, would be a terrific achievement in the camellia world. I can't wait to see the reaction from my camellia friends when the cross potential of these two different camellias are realized.

Meanwhile, Longwood Gardens has been crossing *Camellia azalea* with the cold-hardy *Camellia japonica* 'Maiden of Great Promise', and they say the results so far show great promise as compatible breeding partners.

Just when you think you have heard the latest in camellias (the *Camellia azalea*) something new arouses the camellia world. Gao Jiyin, who wrote about the *Camellia azalea* in the *International Camellia Journal* has now written about the discovery of a unique, ever-blooming yellow camellia treasure named *Camellia chuangtsoensis*. Gao and a group of scientists traveled some 620 miles from Guangdong Province to Guangi autonomous region in 2007. Upon arriving in the region they climbed a steep mountain and were finally rewarded by finding a colony of six-foot camellias with "green, shiny, leathery leaves producing deep yellow . . . pure gold colored flowers."

The new species was found to have similarities with camellia azalea in fruit, flowers, and tenderness. This past year Professor Gao and his associates have already crossed 600 flowers of *Camellia azalea* with the *Camellia chuangtsoensis*. It was determined the best use of the new species will be in "breeding new, ever-blooming cultivars."

Both of my Georgia camellia expert friends, Mark Crawford and Gene Phillips, were excited about the new find, agreeing it opens many future opportunities for hybridizing. Mark, however, said that Longwood Gardens confirms that it will be difficult to get the plant out of China, prompting him to rebuke the editor of the *Camellia Journal* for featuring a plant find that will be unavailable to the American Camellia Society. Gene said, "This country is just beginning to understand the *Camellia azalea* and therefore is a long way from understanding this new yellow species." However, Gene would like to someday cross the new species with a large white *C. japonica* with the aim of giving it the cold hardiness needed for our zone 7. Encouraging in the pursuit of this future goal is the fact my other Georgia camellia expert Hulyn Smith reports that foliage of the new species is more like *C. japonica*. I will be watching with special interest as my passionate camellia friends pursue and track yet another new exciting species.

I have enjoyed getting to know the camellia lovers, most of whom have grown up with the genus all of their life. Their passion is contagious. They call the camellia "the queen of the ornamentals" and will tell you they date back to 5000 BC, native to Japan, China, and Southeast Asia. The tea camellia (*C. sinensis*) was brought to the American colonies in the 1700s as a possible agriculture crop, but it was not successful. (I have a cluster of these fall, white-blooming species in my garden.) However, afterward, the craze began, and now they can be found outside or in greenhouses throughout the country. Camellias can live a long time, and some in Charleston date back more than 200 years.

The best advice that was ever given to me, and that I enthusiastically pass on, is to pursue something that you enjoy doing. Success—defined as doing the best you can do in whatever you pursue—is best achieved by enjoying and being passionate about your work. I was fortunate to have done that, and the people I have met in the camellia world, and to a large extent the horticulture world, are examples of such passion.

ENDOWED PROFESSORSHIP

One of the many friends I made in the nursery business was a University of Georgia horticulture graduate by the name of Bill Reynierson. His interest in the Georgia Bulldogs and mine in horticulture were a mutual draw. Bill had great admiration for Dr. Dirr, who he stated was "instrumental in fostering his development as a student and a businessman." He discussed with me making a tangible gift for a scholarship. Out of that idea and Bill's seed gift came the plan to raise $250,000 for an endowment professorship in Dirr's name. The idea was music to the ears of the horticulture department and the College of Agricultural and Environmental Science, because the

University of Georgia, like other public institutions throughout the country, was changing its culture from receiving state financial support to raising it. State funding for higher education over the past two decades has been on a downward spiral, which prompted a culture change to fund-raising.

Because I had been involved in the initial plans, I agreed to lead the charge primarily out of my admiration of Dr. Dirr. I also felt I was well qualified since the culture of athletic funding had changed during my tenure of athletic director to an emphasis on fund-raising as well. Football had long supported our entire athletic program, but a desire to expand our sports to be competitive nationally in all sports, especially women's sports and Title IX compliance, necessitated us to become involved in fundraising. As the athletic director I was out front, and that experience I knew would help me in securing funds for the Dirr Professorship.

Because of the esteem in which Dr. Dirr was held in the industry, it was an easy sell. Gifts ranging from $5,000 to $50,000 among Dirr followers enabled me to fund the $250,000 professorship in less than a year. The purpose of the fund was "to perpetuate the work and influence" of Dr. Dirr in a "future faculty member to serve the industry and embody the commitment to teaching, research and woody plant introductions." Commitments came from such noted nursery people as J. Guy, Skeeter McCorkle, Mike Glenn, John Barber, and Tommy and Mike Dudley. Tommy and Mike are rabid Bulldogs of Dudley Nursery in Thomson, Georgia, who grew the "sons and daughters" of the Hedges (II) during the Centennial Olympics.

Two of the more interesting asks I encountered came from Fred Hooks and Richard Vanlandingham of Wight Nursery in Cairo. I asked Fred if he would consider a $25,000 lead gift, and he said no but he would like to make a $50,000 gift. I was pleasantly stunned! It was a great example in the fund-raising business of the old saying "Never underask." The second memorable gift came after a $25,000 ask to Richard Vanlandingham, who said, "Yes, I will give $25,000 for the Dirr professorship, but I also want to give $25,000 to establish the Allan Armitage professorship, who has done so much for the herbaceous plant industry." Thus was born the Allan M. Armitage endowed professorship for herbaceous plant instruction and introduction.

The development office of the college took the $25,000 for the Armitage professorship and ran with it, contacting nurseries that specialize in annuals and perennials. I was asked to help, which I gladly did by speaking to seminar groups and making an occasional trip to nurseries such as Louis Stacy's nursery in York, South Carolina, who made a generous gift. The endowment, like Dr. Dirr's, perpetuates Armitage's work and influence in the horticulture industry in America. The professorship for the instruction and introduction of herbaceous plants parallels Armitage's saying that "new plants are the lifeblood of the horticulture industry."

When I retired from the university, the athletic association funded a professorship in the horticulture department in my name. I was proud to say at the time that there were only three endowed professorships in the College of Agricultural and Environmental Science, all three in the horticulture department, and I was directly involved in all three of them. Realistically the professorships are a tribute to the high esteem in which my mentors Dr. Armitage and Dr. Dirr are held. In football lingo, they are the Herschel Walkers of the industry; but on the other hand, like Herschel, you have to give them the ball to produce.

CHAPTER EIGHT

THE
DOOLEY SCULPTURE
GARDEN

THE DOOLEY SCULPTURE GARDEN
AT THE UNIVERSITY OF GEORGIA

I am a little torn writing about a statue and a garden in my honor. However, despite my reservation of being the focal point, the garden and the sculpture are extraordinary, and the efforts by the people responsible for making it happen were also extraordinary.

Stan Mullins, who received his undergraduate and master's in art at the university, and Russ Thornton, another Georgia graduate whose late father, Jack, once played for me, conceived the idea (over libation) of a statue in my honor. From that inauspicious beginning the project took a circuitous four-year journey that has been captured in a book by the talented artist Stan "the Art Man" Mullins entitled *The Making of a Champion*. The twisted journey would still be ongoing had it not been for the initiative of three distinguished Georgians—Senator Johnny Isakson, Billy Payne, and the university systems chancellor Earl Davis. Their endorsements put the project on a fast track, and the plan was approved by the university's administration, faculty, and athletic association and the state board of regents.

Stan calls his bronze sculpture "the character of a champion," and despite the subject, it is remarkable. The fifteen-foot, two-ton bronze statue

Albizia julibrissin 'Pendula'
Weeping Mimosa Tree

depicts two Georgia linemen carrying the ol' coach on their shoulders after a big victory during the 1980 national championship season. The pedestal, made of blue Pennsylvania granite, is three feet tall and weighs some nine tons! The statue was funded, under the leadership of Billy Payne, by seven other longtime friends and university supporters. The athletic association funded the entire garden area.

The decision was made to erect the statue and garden on the corner of the South entrance to the campus next to the athletic complex. I was pleased since it converted an unattractive grass slope into a beautiful south entrance to the campus.

In a brief meeting with the university planning committee and the architect, Gary Coursey, my only request was for the landscape architect to seek Armitage's and Dirr's advice before installing any plants. Armitage was on a sabbatical and was eventually consulted about herbaceous color. However, Dirr spoke up immediately, saying he didn't want any "meatballs or lettuce" in the garden. He insisted on specimen plants, the cutting-edge type not found in most gardens.

Dirr suggested we meet the landscape architect, Alex Maddox, in Hickory, North Carolina, at Hawksridge Nursery to discuss plant selection with highly regarded

nurseryman Rick Crowder. The specimen plants selected from Hawksridge Nursery formed the basis of the Maddox-designed garden that covers almost an acre.

There are three distinct levels in the entire garden and eleven distinct garden areas. Ironically the garden is approximately the length (a hundred yards) and the width (fifty-three and a half yards) of a football field. Within that space are, surprisingly, 16 large trees, 48 small trees, and some 745 shrubs. There are also 250 perennial flowers and 370 annuals for seasonal color, along with 17 vines and 610 grasses throughout the garden. To my amazement the total number of plants and trees is over 2,055! Don't worry, I will not be naming them all, though I will elaborate here on my favorite separate garden and a few extraordinary new plants. Incidentally, can you imagine digging 2,055 holes? And in two days—the time it took to install the garden.

I am proud the sculpture garden will be an asset to the campus for generations to come. A special reward is the longtime educational use that will be available for the students and the faculty of horticulture, landscape architecture, and art as an outdoor laboratory.

In addition, the garden will serve as an oasis to draw people in general for reflection or respite. This is especially true in the sanctuary of the weepers garden, my favorite place in the park.

THE WEEPING CONTEMPLATIVE GARDEN

Guarding the entrance to the weeping contemplative garden are two 'Hearts of Gold' redbuds (*Cercis canadensis*) that light up the sky with their newly flushed bright gold leaves in the spring. Oval shaped, somewhat like a football, the area is about twenty yards (two first downs) long and ten yards (a first down) wide. In the garden are seven small weeping trees that encircle four flat concrete benches, ideally suited for viewing and contemplating.

Prunus subhirtella 'Pendula'
Weeping Cherry

Vince Dooley in the Contemplative Garden

Upon entering the garden, just to the left, is a unique weeping mimosa tree (*Albizia julibrissin* 'Pendula'). Following the mimosa is a weeping cherry (*Prunus subhirtella* 'Pendula') and a weeping river birch (*Betula nigra* 'Summer Cascade'), and located at the far end of the oval-shaped garden, next to the wall, is the only large upright tree, a lacebark Chinese elm (*Ulmus parvifolia* Allèe®). To the right of the elm is one of the all-time best weeping Japanese maples (*Acer palmatum* var. *dissectum atropurpureum* 'Tamukeyama'). Rounding the narrow curve is a weeping winged elm (*Ulmus alata* 'Lace Parasol'), a weeping Katsura tree (*Cercidiphyllum japonicum* 'Amazing Grace'), and located back at the entrance, a weeping baldcypress (*Taxodium distichum* 'Cascade Falls').

Serving as understories to the weepers are some of the more recent dwarf plant introductions grouped in mass, complementing the overlooking weepers. *Viburnum obovatum* 'Reifler's Dwarf' is a delightful plant with dark leaves and abundant white flowers. *Spiraea japonica* 'Little Princess', with deep pink flowers, has been a consistent winner. *Hypericum kalmianum* Blue Velvet™ (St. John's Wort), an introduction by my friend Paul Cappiello, has beautiful slender blue green leaves. *Rhaphiolepis umbellata*

minor 'Gulf Green' Indian hawthorne is an attractive plant with a compact upright growth habit with white fragrant flowers in the spring.

A SELECTED FEW

Ten other small gardens complete the garden complex, each with a variety of interesting plants that will be putting their best feet forward during various times of the year. Periodic strolls are the best way to savor the delightful palette of trees, plants, and flowers that grace the park. While all the plants are special, a few of the newest and most distinctive plants deserve extra attention.

Coming out of the weepers garden on the left, shining brightly on a mound near the wall of the statue plaza, is one of the best-looking pines I have ever seen. It is one of the newest Japanese red pines (*Pinus densiflora*) called 'Burke's Red Variegated'. This is another form of the better-known 'Dragon Eye' pine, showing brilliant yellow-banded needles. Another one of these handsome specimens stands to the right of the weepers garden and the stairway from the statue plaza. Next to the yellow pine is a green cousin, an attractive Japanese black pine (*Pinus*

THE SCULPTURE GARDEN

1. Sculpture Plaza
2. Weeping Contemplative Garden
   a. *Cercis canadensis* 'Hearts of Gold'
      Eastern Redbud
   b. *Albizia julibrissin* 'Pendula'
      Mimosa
   c. *Prunus subhirtella* 'Pendula'
      Higan Cherry
   d. *Betula nigra* 'Summer Cascade'
      River Birch
   e. *Ulmus parvifolia* Allèe®
      Chinese Elm
   f. *Acer palmatum* var. *dissectum atropurpureum* 'Tamukeyama'
      Japanese Maple
   g. *Ulmus alata* 'Lace Parasol'
      Winged Elm
   h. *Cercidiphyllum japonicum* 'Amazing Grace'
      Katsuratree
   i. *Taxodium distichum* 'Cascade Falls'
      Common Baldcypress
3. Tribute Plaque
   Annual color
4. *Cryptomeria japonica* 'Little Diamond'
   Dwarf Japanese Cedar

5. *Camellia* hybrid 'High Fragrant'
   Japanese Camellia
6. *Hydrangea macrophylla* 'Dooley'
   Bigleaf Hydrangea
7. *Pinus densiflora* 'Burke's Red Pine'
   Japanese Red Pine
8. *Nyssa sylvatica* 'Autumn Cascades'
   Black Tupelo
9. *Nyssa sylvatica* Red Rage™ ('Hayman Red')
   Black Tupelo
10. *Osmanthus heterophyllus* 'Sasaba'
    Holly Tea-olive
11. *Pinus thunbergii*
    Japanese Black Pine
12. *Muhlenbergia capillaris*
    Muehly grass
13. *Acer palmatum* var. *dissectum* 'Germaine's Gyration'
    Japanese Maple
14. *Rosa* Knock Out® 'Radrazz'
    Knock Out® Rose
15. *Chionanthus retusus* 'Tokyo Tower'
    Chinese Fringetree
16. *Morus australis* 'Unryu'
    Corkscrew Mulberry

17. *Acer palmatum* 'Sango Kaku'
    Japanese Maple
18. *Nyssa sylvatica* 'Wildfire'
    Black Tupelo
19. *Lagerstroemia* hybrid Cherry Dazzle™
    Common Crapemyrtle
20. *Gardenia jasminoides* 'Crown Jewel'
    Gardenia
21. . *Acer palmatum* 'Bihou'
    Japanese Maple
22. *Hydrangea arborescens* 'Annabelle'
    Smooth Hydrangea
23. *Zelkova serrata* 'Ogon'
    Japanese Zelkova
24. *Illicium parviflorum* 'Florida Sunshine'
    Small Anise Tree
25. *Cornus officinalis*
    Japanese Cornel Dogwood
26. *Camellia sasanqua* ×c. *vernalis* 'Yuletide'
    Sasanqua Camellia
27. *Osmanthus* ×*burkwoodii*
    Compact hybrid Tea Olive

thunbergii). The statue plaza stairways are tastefully lined with one of the newest and best dwarf Japanese cedars (*Cryptomeria japonica* 'Little Diamond'). The soft, light-green foliage of this dwarf gem provides an attractive entrance border to the statue plaza.

Strolling up the garden away from the statue plaza, one finds a new and unique Japanese maple (*Acer palmatum* var. *dissectum*) 'Germaine's Gyration'. It is a green dissectum that reaches a height of eight feet but has a spread of twelve feet. The uniqueness is the twisted branches (gyrations) that form a broad mound with a beautiful red-orange fall color.

In the same area are several tea olives (*Osmanthus heterophyllus* 'Sasaba'). This interesting and unique looking cultivar with dark-green, stiff, sharp, spiny leaves is called by Dr. Dirr "a plant handler's worst nightmare." Wisely, my friend Ron Deal, who installed the plants, put them next to the wall of the sculpture plaza out of harm's way to visitors and/or curious gardeners.

While speaking of these fragrant, white-flowered tea olives, I should mention *Osmanthus ×burkwoodii* with a compact habit, lustrous dark green leaves, and fragrant white flowers in March. The only downside is it is hard to find in the garden. Ron chose to plant the six dwarf tea olives in the extreme upper corner of the east upper level (I may move them), thereby assuring they will have no visitors except perhaps my good friend Willis Hardin, who supplied the shrubs. Willis is a highly respected nurseryman from nearby Commerce, Georgia, who loves the plant and is one of the few who carry the species. Barbara and I have visited Willis and his delightful wife, Betty, on several occasions in their lake-house garden to view their spectacular rhododendron collection (the best I have ever seen) in bloom.

Three handsome *Zelkova serrata* (Japanese zelkova) 'Ogon' are spaced along the east-west walkway. This slow-growing cultivar has rich yellow leaves in the spring and

Zelkova serrata 'Ogon'
Japanese Zelkova

yellow-green leaves in summer and fall. The stems are brownish yellow, but the striking feature is the handsome burnt-orange bark. Also along the west end of the sidewalk are several attention-getters, including five double Knock Out® roses developing thick canopies perched on a standard single trunk. Another head turner, along the west-end sidewalk, is the shapely twisted stems of a contorted mulberry (*Morus australis* 'Unryu'), a Barbara favorite. There is also a weeping black tupelo *Nyssa sylvatica* 'Autumn Cascades' at the end of the west sidewalk.

Also along the sidewalk, at the east end, planted in the middle of a small circular garden surrounded by several dwarf Crapemyrtle (Cherry Dazzle™), is a black tupelo (*Nyssa sylvatica* 'Wildfire'). This cultivar is very showy, with its "bronze-red to reddish-purple new shoots." This attractive specimen, however, takes second place to the *Nyssa* cultivar Red Rage™ ('Hayman Red'), located near the footpath by the statue plaza. Dirr calls this cultivar, introduced by Mike Hayman (a fellow traveler on the England garden tour) of Louisville, Kentucky, "the best selection to date" with "superb red fall color."

The Cherry Dazzle™ (*Lagerstroemia indica*) that surrounds the tupelo is the best of the dwarf "Razzle Dazzle"

Acer palmatum 'Sango Kaku', bark color intensifies in winter
Japanese Maple

Lagerstroemia indica Cherry Dazzle™
Crapemyrtle

crapemyrtle series by Dirr and his team, introduced by McCorkle Nurseries, Inc. in Dearing, Georgia. Speaking of McCorkle Nursery, I would be remiss not to mention Heaven Scent™ gardenia, one of the latest introductions by this excellent nursery. There are several in the sculpture garden, but most of the gardenias are 'Crown Jewel'. These compact repeat bloomers along the garden walkway next to the iron fence produce intoxicating, aromatic blooms throughout the spring.

As previously mentioned, there are too many specimen plants in the sculpture garden to mention them all. However, a few more selected favorites are worthy of discussion. In the upper level of the northeast corner, twelve *Illicium parviflorum* 'Florida Sunshine' (Anise tree) light up the area all year with their bright yellow leaves. Close by are a couple of Japanese cornel dogwoods (*Cornus officinalis*) that are "a thing of beauty" when the yellow star-like flowers appear before the leaves in March and April. Directly below on the second level are fifteen of the very popular *Hydrangea arborescens* 'Annabelle' that come into full glory in June-July with their large white snowball flowers.

On the third level adjacent to the Georgia track com-

prising an area of about 180 square feet are a variety of ornamental grasses. The highlight is the showy Muehly grass (*Muehlenbergia capillaris*), whose "light, airy" purple flowers sway in the wind and grab everyone's attention in the fall.

By far the newest and most interesting and fascinating plant in the entire garden is a Japanese maple (*Acer palmatum* 'Bihou'). First of all, it is the most expensive plant in the garden because it is the most sought after and least available. It is certainly the most talked about, and a couple of quotes off the Internet by some plant aficionados will give you a flavor of the cravings for this new cultivar: "I am drooling over this one . . . where can I find it?" "I never believed in love at first sight until I saw this maple." One nurseryman described 'Bihou' as this "outrageous new Japanese maple with vivid coral-orange stems in winter with an upright vase-shaped character with tiny yellow-green leaves in the summer turning orange in the fall." The most distinguished characteristic is the bark color in the winter. All agree it is "vivid and stunning" but don't agree on the color description, which ranges from "orange-yellow" to "coral-yellow" to "orange" to "yellow" to "orange-peach" and finally "golden-yellow peach," which would be my description.

However, I would add yellow bark with alternating yellow and coral stems as a further description. I have 'Bihou', which means "beautiful mountain range" in Japanese, planted next to the fence that overlooks two terraced gardens and the Georgia track.

Those enthusiastic maple people from the United States that have been in search of this maple can now get the plant from All Things Acer nursery in Winchester, Tennessee, a new maple nursery founded by the renowned Don Shadow and Fred Hooks, who have introduced the plant into the United States. It started out as a seedling from Japan and spread to France before making its way to the good ol' USA.

After writing about the cost and the beauty of 'Bihou', a plant alarm or armed guard around this rare elegant aristocrat is worth considering.

The striking yellow color of 'Bihou' is complemented by the brilliant coral fall and winter color of the barks and stems of the two ten- to twelve-foot 'Sango Kaku' (*Acer palmatum*) Japanese maples. The three distinctive maples, spaced about five yards apart, are aligned in the center of the garden and look like colorful soldiers on duty in their "dress coral and/or yellow" uniforms guarding the park. It makes for a very attractive winter show.

The fall-winter garden show is concluded with two of the most popular camellias in the South. The first is the versatile 'Yuletide', (*C. ×vernalis*). This cultivar, which is a cross between *C. japonica* and *C. sasanqua*, will take full sun or shade and produce beautiful single red flowers with bright yellow stamens. The flowers will last from October to January. There are four 'Yuletide' located next to the far east wall on the upper level of the garden.

Next to the far east wall abutting the statue plaza, three *Camellia* hybrids, 'High Fragrant', are located. This cultivar is the best of the fragrant camellia hybrids. The sweet-scented, pink peony-form flowers that open in February provide a welcome addition to the winter garden. While researching the hybrid, it was interesting to learn that Mr. James Finley of New Zealand has been working on fragrant camellias for over twenty years and has produced several that are on the market. The infusion of fragrance into camellias has elevated the spirit of the camellia lovers, causing one to quip, "Now winter-blooms offer everything the summer rose does, except thorns!" The learning journey continues.

I am appreciative of all the work by so many that had a hand in making the sculpture garden an educational showplace. I am also appreciative of a plaque that was installed (to my humble and complete surprise) in the middle of the garden in the plaza bench area that contains the following tribute:

> This garden depicts Coach Dooley's interest and commitment to horticulture. Many of the plants selected are his personal favorites and some of the plants were transplanted from his Athens home. The "Dooley Hydrangea" and the "Vince Dooley Camellia" were named in his honor and he was instrumental in the University's campus being designated as an arboretum. Coach Dooley was presented Georgia Urban Forest Council's 2000 Individual Achievement Award given for significant accomplishments in promoting urban forestry in Georgia.

Whoever is responsible, thanks!

CHAPTER NINE

THE DOOLEY HOME GARDEN

MINI BOTANICAL GARDEN

My garden has often been called a mini botanical garden, and that is probably an apt description. Over the past fifteen years, my quest for plants and trees, many acquired from Dr. Dirr's experimental throwaway collection plus the generosity of a lot of nursery friends, has enabled me to assemble a wide variety of plant life with many new and unusual cultivars. The garden contains a large number of native azaleas, magnolias, and viburnums and an even larger number of hydrangeas, camellias, and Japanese maples. There are over one hundred plants of named and unnamed hydrangea cultivars and approximately 120 varieties of camellias throughout the garden, as well as about forty more that are duplications. Likewise, there are about 120 Japanese maple cultivars plus an additional fifty unnamed seedlings.

Despite the large numbers and wide diversity of plant life, there is one well-known tree I do not have, nor desire to acquire. It is the popular but somewhat notorious Bradford pear (*Pyrus calleryana* 'Bradford'). If I had ever acquired one, Dirr would never let me live it down. The tree, however, is an interesting paradox.

In the last quarter century, the popularity of the tree enabled it to inhabit cities and towns throughout the country, reaching, as Dirr has described, "epidemic proportions." Serious weaknesses have been discovered over a period of time, such as severe limb splitting and undesirable fruit, not to mention the foul smell of the white flowers that cover the tree in early spring. Dirr has seen so many of these overplanted specimens around the country he once told me they were "short of a biological sin." I love his whimsical characterizations. However, he does admit the leaf color is "outstanding" and the fall color is "spectacular." As for me, I will admire its assets from afar, I'll just have another Japanese maple.

I have earlier discussed some of the expert hydrangea and camellia friends I have met. Fred Hooks ranks right at the top among the Japanese maple experts and is the master of accumulating new introductions of those aristocratic marvels. While on the subject I should also mention my friend Mike Francis at Maple Ridge Nursery in East Atlanta, whose love and passion for Japanese maples has moved him to accumulate an endless variety with some rare coveted treasures. I have visited his nursery on several occasions, always leaving with a few new varieties. I asked him one day for a catalog, and he smiled and said that his catalog is J. D. Vertrees's book on Japanese maples. Vertrees's book is regarded as the best Japanese maple book in existence. I have often said that I have never met a Japanese maple I didn't like. There is an endless variety of sizes, shapes, forms, and colors, and Mike Francis seems to either have them all or is in the process of securing them.

COACH PAT DYE

Speaking of securing Japanese maples, I recently visited my friend and former coaching rival Pat Dye, who upon retiring from coaching at Auburn University several years ago bought a 700-plus-acre farm nearby. To my amazement, I found Pat had purchased several hundred Japanese maples to add to the couple hundred he already had. We share a common love of these aristocrats, and we both grow them for pleasure. The similarities stop there, because in addition to pleasure, Pat is growing them for profit. He is in the business of selling Japanese maples at his recently completed Quail Hollow Nursery and Garden outside Auburn, Alabama.

Pat is the only other college football coach I know of who has been bitten by the horticulture bug. We share a lot in common in coaching, both taking similar paths but in opposite directions. I played football at Auburn and coached there before coming to Georgia to coach, eventually making Athens and the university my permanent home. Pat played football at Georgia and later became the successful head coach at Auburn before making the area in east Alabama his permanent home. One could say we both have two loves, but the romances happened at different times. This unique situation remains today somewhat baffling to the alumni of each institution. Only Pat and I can fully understand.

We also share the fact we grew up in hard times, but in different environments. I was a city boy growing up during the Depression near downtown Mobile, Alabama. Pat grew up a few years later on the family farm in Blythe, Georgia, in the eastern part of the state, near Augusta. He was, and still is, a farm boy at heart, working the farm and first driving a tractor at age ten. Since his retirement he has driven every piece of farm equipment known to man. He has planted and moved trees, thinned pines, and ground stumps, all the while falling in love with Japanese maples. His first loves are the two huge ones he planted near his house several years ago.

He recently purchased the entire Japanese maple stock from Fox McCarthy of Fox Hollow Nursery in

ACER PALMATUM CULTIVARS IN THE DOOLEY GARDEN

'Ryusen'

'Beni Shishihengé'

'Mikawa Yatsubusa'

'Inaba Shidara' with St. Francis

'Oshio Beni'

'Waterfall'

'Butterfly'

'Katsura'

'Orangeola'

THE DOOLEY HOME GARDEN

1. Driveway Stroll
2. *Camellia sasanqua* Walk
3. *Acer palmatum* var. *dissectum atropurpureum* 'Tamukeyama'
   Japanese Maple
4. *Cornus kousa* 'Lustgarten Weeping'
   Kousa Dogwood
5. Encore® Hybrids (Azalea)
6. *Cercis canadensis* Collection
   Eastern Redbud
7. *Prunus serrulata* 'Kwanzan'
   Japanese Flowering Cherry
8. *Prunus mume* 'Dawn'
   Flowering Apricot
9. *Rosa* Knock Out® ('Radrazz')
   Knock Out® Rose
10. *Loropetalum chinense* var. *rubrum* 'Burgundy'
    Chinese Fringe-flower
11. *Ilex vomitoria*
    Yaupon Holly
12. *Magnolia ×loebneri* 'Leonard Messel'
    Loebner Magnolia
13. *Hydrangea macrophylla* 'Dooley'
    Bigleaf Hydrangea
14. Perennial Garden
    a. *Baptisia australis*
       False Blue Indigo
    b. *Rudbeckia hirta*
       Black-Eyed Susan
15. *Chionanthus virginicus*
    White Fringetree
16. *Aesculus parviflora*
    Bottlebrush Buckeye
17. *Acer griseum ×Acer maximowiczianum*
    Paperbark Maple ×Nikko Maple
18. *Acer palmatum* 'Sango Kaku'
    Coral Bark Japanese Maple
19. *Acer palmatum* var. *dissectum atropurpureum* 'Red Cutleaf'
    Japanese Maple
20. *Acer palmatum* var. *atropurpureum* 'Oshio Beni'
    Japanese Maple
21. *Lagerstroemia* hybrid 'Sarah's Favorite'
    Crapemyrtle
22. Ryan's Memorial Patio Container Garden
23. *Ulmus parvifolia* Allee® ('Emer II')
    Chinese or Lacebark Elm
24. *Corylus avellana* 'Contorta' (Harry Lauder's Walking Stick)
    European Filbert
25. *Wisteria sinensis* 'Augusta Pride'
    Chinese Wisteria
26. *Cornus kousa* var. *angustata* Empress of China® ('Elsbry')
    Kousa Dogwood
27. *Helleborus orientalis*
    Lenten Rose
28. *Rhododendron austrinum* ×Exbury 'Hotspur Yellow' 'Admiral Semmes'
    Confederate Series Hybrid (Azalea)
29. *Thuja orientalis* 'Aurea'
    Oriental Arborvitae
30. Perennial Garden
31. *Cedrus atlantica* 'Glauca'
    Atlas Cedar
32. *Metasequoia glyptostroboides*
    Dawn Redwood
33. *Acer palmatum* var. *dissectum* 'Seiryu'
    Japanese Maple
34. Weepers Corner
35. The Shade Garden
36. *Magnolia stellata*
    Star Magnolia
37. *Koelreuteria paniculata*
    Panicled Goldenraintree
37a. Rustic Bridge Crossing
38. Camellia Walk
39. Rock Garden
40. *Viburnum macrocephalum*
    Chinese Snowball Viburnum
41. *Acer palmatum* 'Katsura'
    Japanese Maple
42. *Hydrangea macrophylla* Endless Summer® ('Bailmer')
    Bigleaf Hydrangea
43. *Cornus capitata* 'Mountain Moon'
    Evergreen Dogwood
44. Weepers Creek
45. *Taxodium distichum* 'Cascade Falls'
    Weeping Baldcypress
46. *Cercidiphyllum japonicum* 'Amazing Grace'
    Katsura Tree
47. *Magnolia grandiflora*
    Southern Magnolia
48. *Aucuba japonica*
    Japanese Aucuba
49. The Fountain Circle Walk
    a. *Hydrangea macrophylla* 'Mini Penny'
       Bigleaf Hydrangea
50. *Buxus sempervirens*
    American Boxwood
51. *Morus alba*
    Common Mulberry
52. *Rhododendron*
    Satsuki Hybrid Azalea
53. *Acer palmatum* var. *dissectum atropurpureum* 'Garnet'
    Japanese Maple
54. *Acer palmatum* var. *atropurpureum* 'Bloodgood'
    Japanese Maple

Conyers, Georgia. Fox specializes in field-grown eight-to-ten-foot-high and five-to-nine-foot-spread maples. I've known Fox for several years and purchased a top-of-the-line cascading maple from him called 'Tamukeyama', a wonderful purple dissectum.

Pat has thinned five acres, terraced several elevations, installed modern irrigation, and constructed a beautiful cascading rock waterfall through the middle of his garden. He is in business already selling his maples, but now that the garden is complete, this spectacular showpiece garden is a great incentive to pull people in to view his stock. I am looking forward to a return trip.

Pat, a sharing gardener like all good men of the soil, gave me a Japanese maple *Acer palmatum* 'Bihou'. It is a small version of the one in the sculpture garden, but nevertheless a treasure. When Pat comes to my garden I will reciprocate. This bonding in the soil is a lot better and more fun at this stage of our lives than competing year in and year out in a game that has life-or-death connotations to Auburn and Georgia fans.

A rabid Auburn and Pat Dye man that I have enjoyed knowing in the nursery business is Richard May. Richard is a third-generation man of the soil from Havana, Florida, just outside Tallahassee, where he works in the family nursery with his father, uncles, brother, and cousins. Above anything else, Richard is an Auburn graduate and Tiger football fanatic. I have visited him at his nursery and at trade shows. I talk plants while he talks football—especially Auburn football. Richard has been generous with his plants, and I have several, the most noted of which is a golden-leaf hydrangea that he calls 'Lemonade', a branch sport of the double-flowered mophead 'Domotoi'. I won't be surprised if one day he presents me with a plant that he has called 'War Eagle'.

While reminiscing about men of this lovely village, another Auburn man in the nursery business, the late Arthur "Buck" Jones of Grayson, Georgia, comes to mind. He was one of the most respected nurserymen in the state, and when he died he passed the torch to his daughter, Laurie Fisher, a Georgia horticulture student who was on our gymnastics team. The Auburn-Georgia cross pollination is part of the love of these feuding cousins.

Meanwhile, this Auburn grad who has adopted the Georgia Bulldog keeps up with his many Japanese maples and array of hydrangeas, camellias, viburnums, etc. by routinely taking a lap around the garden after a daily morning workout. Since I have ended up with virtually a garden for all seasons, there is always something different happening when I take my daily stroll. The best way to see the garden is to walk with me. Before doing so, a word about the house is appropriate. All told, we have over two and a half acres of land—about half comprises the garden and the rest consists of an expansive lawn and a house that has survived ten major additions since we moved into the residence in 1965.

The latest addition, a patio room, or sunporch, by Champion Windows, accentuates the garden theme by bringing the house into the garden, providing a spectacular view and place for spiritual reflection. The Colonial revival–style house sits about a hundred yards, or the length of a football field, from the road in a valley framed by two large loblolly pines and rests on a slight rise across from a deep stream forded by a driveway bridge and one rustic-style and two Japanese walking bridges.

A DRIVEWAY STROLL

The most natural way to approach the garden is by walking down the driveway located on the left side facing the house. On the left along the fenced property line that separates a large next-door meadow are several varieties of *Camellia sasanqua* that bloom in the fall at the time we

PENLEY

Rhododendron macrosepalum 'Koromo Shikibu'
Japanese Azalea

traditionally entertained guests during football season. The varieties include 'Shell Pink', 'Setsugekka', 'Cleopatra', 'Martha's Dream', 'Sparkling Burgundy', 'Hana Jiman', the popular white double-flower 'Mine No Yuki' ('White Doves' 'Snow on the Mountain'), 'Pink Snow', and the red, long-blooming 'Yule Tide', especially popular during Christmas season. The camellias are bordered by low, spreading *Cephalotaxus harringtonia* (Japanese Plum Yew) along with clusters of border forsythia and white- and pink-flowering *Loropetalum chinense*. On the right side at the top of the driveway, nestled under a loblolly pine (*Pinus taeda*), is a mixed border of Encore® azaleas, double-pink Knock Out® roses, and variegated Asian beautyberry (*Callicarpa dichotoma* 'Duet'). Of special interest are two weeping, dissected Japanese maples (*Acer palmatum* 'Tamukeyama'), and under one is a groundcover called *Veronica* 'Blue Star' creeper with hundreds of tiny blue star flowers that grab the attention of most everyone who starts a tour of the garden in the spring. The latest addition is a dove tree, *Davidia involucrata* 'Sonoma', that produces flowers at an early age, along with showy white bracts that look like doves or handkerchiefs dancing in the breeze. Around

the dove tree are two rare camellia species, the weeping *C. handelii* and the upright *C. buxifolia*. Both have small stems and small white flowers. A few yards farther down on the right is the popular, deep pink, double-flowering oriental cherry (*Prunus serrulata* 'Kwanzan') that shades a wide variety of the repeat-flowering Encore® azaleas. Farther down on the right and next to the creek is the newest river birch Dura Heat™ (*Betula nigra*), which promises to be the best of all these exfoliating bark cultivars. Adjacent to the river birch is a *Prunus mume* 'Dawn' (flowering apricot) that blooms in late January and early February, displaying beautiful double-pink flowers and providing excitement to the garden during the usual dormant wintertime. In front of the flowering apricot and along the creek is a cluster of shrub Knock Out® roses, and they are indeed *knockouts,* blooming continuously from spring to fall. The roses are relatively disease free and require little attention except admiration. They are the single-bloom variety, but several of the red double-blooming Knock Outs® are seen in the pool area.

Dirr brought me some of these roses long before they were called Knock Out. They had a number, which I believe was 234. Because of their fiery red color, and not knowing they would be named Knock Out®, I gave them the name 'Georgia'. I got my first education on how plants are patented. They have been 'Knock Outs' ever since.

CROSSING THE DRIVEWAY BRIDGE

Crossing the creek on the driveway bridge are several groupings of *Loropetalum*, primarily the pink-flowering and/or purple-foliaged varieties. They serve as an understudy to the three umbrella-shaped Yaupon hollies (*Ilex vomitoria*). Between two of the Yaupons is the first of many deciduous magnolias throughout the garden, and perhaps the best of all, *Magnolia* ×*loebneri* 'Leonard Messel'. The twelve-foot small tree produces an abundance of pink-white fragrant flowers. To the right, adjacent to the house, is a large *Hydrangea macrophylla* labeled 'Dooley' by Dr. Dirr. After watching the plant respond to two late freezes in 1996 and 1998 by blooming afterward, he became fascinated with the cold-hardiness of the cultivar as well as its fine texture and large, beautiful, light blue flower heads. The hydrangeas are shaded by a Japanese loquat (*Eriobotrya japonica*).

At the end of the driveway is a diverse perennial garden that features one of Armitage's favorites—*Baptisia australis* (false indigo) in both the purple and gold flower form—as well as *Rudbeckia hirta*, another favorite especially since its common name is 'Black-Eyed Susan'. Armitage's wife's name is Susan. Armitage calls it a "welcome wanderer," and indeed it is, blooming for six solid weeks in the summer. In the background are several *Camellia japonica* and a *Chionanthus virginicus*, or "fringe tree," flanked by a beautiful bottlebrush buckeye (*Aesculus parviflora*), a top native favorite of Dirr's.

To the left of the perennial garden is a stately upright European hornbeam (*Carpinus betulus* 'Fastigiata'), and just to the right are two evergreen oriental *Viburnum awabuki* called 'Chindo', originally discovered on the Chindo Island, Korea, and noted for producing large, pendulous, red fruit clusters. Alongside is a red-flowering mountain laurel (*Kalmia latifolia* 'Sarah'). To the right of the perennial garden is a Japanese stewartia (*Stewartia pseudocamellia*). This magnificent small tree has outstanding bark and white cup-shaped camellia-like flowers. Dirr has expressed reservations about it performing well in Athens (zone 7), but mine has been in place seven years and is performing well so far.

Behind the perennial garden is a cluster of 'Dooley' hydrangea nestled on a small knoll that is covered with *Helleborus orientalis* (Lenten Rose). Located next to a small knee-high-stacked-stone wall are two 'Paper Bush' plants

(*Edgeworthia chrysantha*) that provide clusters of small cream-yellow flowers with great fragrance when in bloom in February, when many other plants are sleeping. Next to the *Edgeworthia* is a cluster of bottlebrush buckeyes (*Aesculus parviflora*) flanked by a purple Encore® azalea called 'Autumn Royalty', which is the best and most robust of the repeat bloomers.

There is also a perennial garden along the driveway to the left containing two *Lagerstroemia indica* 'Natchez', white-flowering crape myrtle with beautiful brown-to-cinnamon exfoliating bark. There are a few more *Camellia sasanqua* 'Rosea' and the pink 'Jean May' producing abundant beautiful flowers in late October. Among the perennials are Japanese asters and Japanese anemones that constantly show their beautiful faces every spring. The narrow driveway garden also contains a fast-growing paperbark maple hybrid with a cinnamon flake-like bark that Dr. Dirr enjoys checking out each time he walks the garden. The hybrid cross is *Acer griseum* × *Acer maximowiczianum* (what a name!) or Paperbark maple × Nikko maple. The orange red fall color and the cinnamon flaking bark are outstanding features.

THE POOL GARDEN

To the right of the driveway, an iron gate leads into the pool area, which introduces the visitor to a series of Japanese maples that prevail throughout the garden. To the left of the entrance is the newest Dirr hydrangea, a gorgeous pink/blue reblooming lacecap. Bailey's Nursery, who had the naming rights, tagged it Twist-n-Shout™ an obvious marketing, attention-getting name; nevertheless the plant is a real winner. It is such a fantastic bloomer that Josh Kardos called it a "blooming machine." To the left of the hydrangea is a tall, light green leaf Japanese maple 'Sango Kaku' (Coral Bark). To the immediate right is another Japanese maple labeled variety *atropurpureum*

'Red Cutleaf'. Just beyond the gate on the left is a Japanese maple 'Oshio-beni', which has a magnificent red (*beni* is Japanese for red) foliage in the spring and fall. To the immediate right is another small perennial garden that contains a cluster of the dwarf 'Shooting Star' and single-flower gardenias with wonderful fragrance. There is also a cluster of the newly introduced 'Kaleidoscope' *Abelia* that lights up the garden with its yellow gold, variegated, colorful leaves. Also in this small garden that is topped by a crape myrtle called 'Sara's Favorite' is a row of Knock Out® roses. This little area also contains one of my favorite perennials, Japanese aster (*Kalimeris pinnatifida*). I really like this reliable plant with its double white flower and yellow stamens that shows up every summer accompanied by more brothers and sisters than the previous summer. Armitage calls it one of his no-brainer plants that anyone can plant "without fear of failure." That's my kind of plant! When I was taking his class I remember him talking about another no-brainer plant, a yellow flag iris (*Iris pseudacorus*). I immediately went to my beginner's garden and planted it. It was a great confidence builder. It will grow in the water (I have one in the pond) or on dry land (I have it in the circle garden). I like those no-brainer plants, and Armitage has several additional ones I have in the garden.

Earlier I mentioned *Baptisia australis* (False Indigo), *Rudbeckia hirta* (Black-Eyed Susan) and *Helleborus orientalis* (Lenten Rose), all Armitage no-brainer perennials. Another Armitage no-brainer in the perennial garden, which is located at the far side of the pool, is *Dianthus* 'Bath's Pink', founded by Jane Bath of Stone Mountain, Georgia. It is good-looking and easy to grow. Other no-brainers are *Verbena* 'Homestead Purple', *Sedum* 'Autumn Joy', *Veronica* 'Goodness Grows', and *Achillea* 'Coronation Gold' (yarrow) that Armitage said was "raised in 1953 to commemorate the coronation of England's Queen Elizabeth II."

Another no-brainer perennial I seem to forget about each year until it appears is *Helianthus angustifolius* (swamp sunflower). It shoots up about six feet with those bright yellow flowers in late summer, and invariably I ask myself, "What is that?" After the fourth season of not remembering that plant, it is about time I remember the swamp sunflower.

The one no-brainer that is a little confusing to me is *Rudbeckia* 'Goldsturm' (yellow coneflower) that Armitage calls the "no-brainer of no-brainers!" I am familiar with *Echinacea purpurea*, the purple coneflower that is also listed as a no-brainer, that Armitage says is a "close relative of *Rudbeckia*." Now comes *Echinacea paradoxa* (yellow coneflower), the same common name given to *Rudbeckia* 'Goldsturm'. Are you as confused as I am?

What I have found out is that a lot has been going on in the *Echinacea* hybridization world in the last several years. The happenings have been described as "a revolution in coneflowers with a wider range of colors and increased scent." Leading that revolution are the Saul brothers—Bob, Richard, and Bob's wife, Kathy—who in 1998 cofounded ItSaul Nursery with Ozzie Johnson. Their work with hybridization and introducing unique plants, including new coneflower cultivars, has sent "shock waves of delight throughout the gardening world." I remember noted horticulturist John Elsley, my British gentleman friend from Greenwood, South Carolina, and *Helleborus* fame, telling me that "the Saul brothers are way ahead of the curve." I wasn't sure what that meant at the time, but I found out they have a splendid reputation for introducing new plants. I have visited them both at their sales location in "the Swamp" and in Alpharetta and their growing facility in Dahlonega. They have been real leaders in the industry. They have always been highly respected, as evidenced by the fact that they were selected to design 800 plants for the 1996 Centennial Olympics. They have taken on a greater leadership role with

Container Garden

the resurgence of their popularity of genus *Echinacea*.

They have introduced some magnificent cultivars of these sun perennials, such as 'Sundown', 'Sunrise', 'Twilight', 'Paranoia', and many more with a wide range of colors. The most floriferous of all the new introductions on the market is 'Adam Saul' (crazy pink) that is reputed to produce a hundred flowers per plant. I have several in my garden and I will be getting more. The great news is that they are part of the no-brainer family.

GARDEN ADVERSITY

I learned from coaching that if you stay in it long enough, anything that can possibly happen will. We had a football saying—always expect the unexpected! I can now say the same for gardening after experiencing the late Easter freeze of 2007 and the great snowfall of March 2009. The late

Easter freeze played havoc on the new tender leaves of the hydrangeas and Japanese maples. As bad as it was at the time, it was nothing compared to the seven-to-nine inches of large-flake, wet snow that fell in 2009 on just five counties in northeast Georgia: Jackson, Madison, Oconee, Oglethorpe, and Clarke. My yard was a disaster, with downed trees and hundreds of broken pine limbs. In the adjacent Mathis garden, three huge pine trees fell, covering almost a hundred square yards of plants. It was even worse in the patio, where two magnificent Chinese elms were devastated by the weight of the heavy snow. The Chinese elms (*Ulmus parvifolia*)—*Ulmus* the classical Latin name of elm, and *parvifolia* meaning "small leaf"—had been in the patio for over twelve years, providing a pleasant shade canopy when we used to entertain during football season. The elms, a Dirr introduction, labeled Allèe® from the original tree on the Georgia campus, provided not only much-needed shade but beautiful orange, gray, and brown exfoliating bark. Losing those trees made Barbara and me sick. The only person who was sicker was Dirr, who had suggested the trees for the patio.

After I retired and no longer had entertainment responsibilities, I converted the patio area, which once seated over one hundred people, into a massive container garden with over a hundred potted plants. New acquisitions of Japanese maples, camellias, hydrangeas, and other specialty plants are kept there for a period of time to get to know them before putting them out to pasture in the garden. Also in the patio are several bonsai plants that I have experimented with, such as a dawn redwood (*Metasequoia glyptostroboides*), paperbark maple (*Acer griseum*), Japanese maple (*Acer palmatum*), dwarf Chinese juniper (*Juniperus chinensis*), and Kingsville dwarf boxwood grove (*Buxus microphylla* var. *japonica* 'Kingsville'). Bonsai plants are fascinating, but practicing the art is a lifetime obsession.

What is almost unbelievable about the snow disaster is that despite all of the elm limbs that fell on the pots, I did not lose a plant! This was also true in the Mathis garden, where the three huge pines fell. The big decision I faced was what trees I would use to replace the destroyed elms in the patio. It needed to be done as quickly as possible to reestablish much-needed shade, not to mention that my garden was on tour that spring with only a three-week window. Dirr went with me to Select Trees in Oconee County to meet our longtime good friend Mike Glenn, who managed, and now owns, this successful tree farm for many years. Mike has been a longtime Bulldog supporter; his son is the assistant tennis coach under Manuel Diaz. For four hours we looked at various options for the patio, but none could match the improved single-leader Chinese elm that Select Trees developed. I now have two young Allèe® Chinese elms in the patio, and these fast growers should soon provide good shade coverage. Meanwhile, I hope it will be another fifty years before this new improved single leader pruned version gets the ultimate test. I am indebted to my friend Mike for his generosity.

Before leaving the patio, reference should be made to two Dirr gifts that are prominent among the many container plants. One is a unique Japanese maple that I have labeled as Dirr throwaway 'Magic Dancer' (I am now naming plants!). The maple rises six inches, and then the strong leader descends down and out about three feet, so much so that I had to elevate the pot on a ledge to cascade, or otherwise it would scrape the ground. Just recently I put the maple in the ground (it was time) in the same spot cascading to the patio. Dr. Dirr always pays his respects to 'Magic Dancer' when he walks the garden. The last time we passed it in early December we were "wowing" over the spectacular yellow, orange, and bronze fall color.

Several years ago I told Dirr I was looking for two small upright conifers to plant on each side of the steps that would eventually grow to frame the house looking from the patio. Shortly two six-foot pyramidal boxwoods called 'Green Mountain' appeared that are now about eight feet tall. The plant is a cross between the American boxwood (*Buxus sempervirens*) and the cold-hardy Korean (*Buxus microphyllia* var. *insularis*) boxwood and had been in Dirr's experimental garden needing a good home. The two 'Green Mountain' are happy campers guarding the entrance to the patio from the house.

A discussion of the patio container garden would not be complete without some reference to two unique containers I use to fulfill the old philosophy that planters should be showy, colorful, and interesting the whole year long. As mentioned, most of my numerous containers are used for new plant acquisitions of Japanese maples, camellias, hydrangeas, and other specialty plants. To give some year-round color I have chosen two of the largest and most interesting containers for the patio. These Styrofoam copper-colored, bowl-like structures, five feet in diameter and about a foot tall, are the creation of the amazing Sara Duke Groves, the delightful, assertive, horticulturist extraordinaire from Oxford, Georgia. While working for the state and helping Billy Payne and Andrew Young bring the 1996 Centennial Olympics to Atlanta, Sara designed these containers for a floral display for the visiting International Olympic Committee members' site selection visits. After securing the Olympics, the floral display containers were used to add color to the competition sites. We hosted three Olympic events in Athens, and I was able to secure two of Sara's design containers for my patio. I was so impressed with the containers that I kept two after the Olympics. At the time I did not know the background of the pots nor did I have a chance to meet the amazing, scintillating Sara.

There are a lot of fundamentals that go into planting containers for seasonal color, but I use a simple rhythmic philosophy I learned that involves plant separation by categories "thrillers, spillers, and fillers." The philosophy states that each container should have one plant that stands out against all the rest—and that is the "thriller." Then there should be a plant that spills over and drapes down the sides of the container—the "spiller." Lastly come the "fillers" that should bring the whole together by weaving in and out, round and about both the thriller and the spiller.

The bowl containers are ideal for experimenting with thrillers, spillers, and fillers, and I follow the same simple formula for spring, summer, and fall planting, always learning from the previous plantings. The floral display planters are located on either side of the steps and are a welcome entrance to or exit from the patio.

RYAN'S GARDEN

While exiting the container garden patio, on the left is a plaque entitled "Ryan's Garden," the name I have given the patio area. Ryan's Garden is in memory of a very special friend, and the inscription on the plaque tells the story of a young man who possessed a lot of saintly qualities.

RYAN'S GARDEN

~

In Memory of Ryan Lantz Conaway
July 26, 1980–December 7, 2005

Who labored with love in this garden for five years while attending the University of Georgia. He brought to this garden the same special qualities that he brought to all that knew him; love, sensitivity, honor, devotion, a charming innocence, and an infectious smile.
He made this garden a lot brighter and the memory of him and his spirit will always be present here.

~

Vince Dooley
December 25, 2005

To continue the garden walk, come up the steps out of Ryan's Garden back into the pool area. On the right is a potted gold-leaf oakleaf *Hydrangea quercifolia* 'Little Honey', happy under the shade of a fragrant winter hazel (*Corylopsis glabrescens*) whose long, fragrant, yellow drooping flowers are a welcome start to spring in early March. Adjacent to the winter hazel is a contorted European filbert (*Corylus avellana* 'Contorta') referred to as 'Harry Lauder's Walking Stick', that adds a lot of interest to the pool and patio area especially in winter. Next to the contorted filbert is the beautiful Chinese wisteria *Wisteria sinensis* 'Augusta Pride', taken from the original oriental wisteria brought to America by Fruitland Nursery, now the site of the Augusta National Golf Club and the Masters. I have it trained on a metal frame, and it produces beautiful blue violet fragrant flowers in April. Afterward a weekly pruning job is necessary and worth it. Just beyond is an often-changing multicolored Japanese maple seedling from my friend Mary Hardman's old Commerce house that provides shade for several (potted) varieties of fragrant mockorange (*Philadelphus* species). A conspicuous golden form (*Philadelphus coronarius* 'Aurea') is just outside the shade and thanks the sun for its brilliance. Also thanking the sun are the golden potted Japanese red pines (*Pinus densiflora*), one called 'Dragon Eye' and the other 'Aurea', providing year-round interest. On the opposite side of the pool, also in pots, are two specimen favorites: a weeping redbud, *Cercis canadensis* subspecies *texensis* 'Traveller', which is spectacular especially in bloom before the leaves break, and a weeping Japanese maple, 'Orangeola', one of my favorite dissectums with bright orange-red new foliage in the spring. Shading the dynamic potted duo is a handsome Chinese flametree (*Koelreuteria bipinnata*). The beautiful, yellow, upright panicle flowers appear at the start of football season in September and shortly thereafter produce showy pink-to-rose seed capsules. We will meet the better-known relative, the panicled, golden-raintree shortly at the creek crossing.

A step up from the pool, located between two small white-flowered *Camellia sasanqua* 'Silver Dollar', is a recycled, waist-high, wrought-iron gate with a stained-glass tulip design in the middle that defines the structure. The gate is a Ron Deal recycled specialty that was taken from a small, old throwaway outdoor decorative bar I purchased when I first arrived in Athens. Deal really enjoys creative recycling, and we will soon encounter another of his creations during the walk.

Before entering the gate, a respectful salute to the right should be made to a stunning new ten-foot Chinese dogwood (*Cornus kousa* var. *angustata*) 'Empress of China'. This late (early summer) dogwood with star-shaped flowers is spectacular. The plant was introduced by my friend, the talented English plantsman John Elsley, who kindly gave me the plant a few years ago. John resides in Greenwood, South Carolina, where I have visited him on a couple of occasions. John and his wife, Billie, added a glassed leisure room with a wonderful view of their garden. Having a "spot of tea" with John in this delightful setting inspired my adding the Champion Windows sunroom to our house.

John at one time worked with Roy Klehm of Klehm's Song Sparrow Nursery in Avalon, Wisconsin. They run a first-class nursery that offers a wide variety of rare plants. Their specialty is peonies and their collection is second to none. The Wisconsin cool climate (zone 4) is ideal for growing the species.

I visited Roy and John when the *Paeonia* were in bloom, and for miles (just like the tulips of Holland) all you could see were rows upon rows of these spectacular multicolored flowers.

Terrace Garden

They gave me several varieties to test and I have them throughout the garden. While our climate is not ideal, and despite the limited flowering time, the flowers are unequaled. They are wonderful cut flowers and the sheer beauty is unmatched. In my opinion, the only other plant that produces flowers as beautiful might be the *Dahlia*. Their beauty and cut-flower performance earned the dahlias the name the "paeonies of the fall." If I had to pick two flowers to grow with ideal growing conditions it would be paeonies and dahlias.

Before leaving the pool garden I would be remiss not to mention a few of the butterfly bushes (*Buddleia davidii*) that have been a mainstay in my garden from the beginning. The main reason of course is that Dirr has done extensive work with *Buddleia* and has shared many of his introductions with me. I have had white, lavender, pink, red, yellow, and many in-between colors of this wonderful summer-flowering species that does indeed attract numerous butterflies. In Dirr's latest study, he said he "took notes on 103 cultivars and passed on others." I like all I have met, always finding a spot for a new one. I have the blue-purple form located at the entrances of both the terraced and perennial gardens.

Walking through the tulip gate leads to the terraced garden. A two-level flat area is raised and held by stacked stones. The garden area was formed by removing some fifty feet of an *Elaeagnus pungens* hedge. There is still enough of the hedge left, providing a nice fragrance in the fall, proving that this plant, often referred to as "Ugly Agnes," has some redeeming qualities. This terraced garden features two 'Annabelle' hydrangeas and a variety of native azalea hybrids developed by Tommy Dodd of Mobile. The hybrid crosses the heat-resistant *Rhododendron austrinum* with the large-flowered Exbury azalea 'Hotspur Yellow' to form the "Confederate Series." There are a variety of cultivars bearing such names as 'Robert E. Lee', 'Stonewall Jackson', and 'Admiral Semmes'. Admiral Semmes, proven to be the best of the hybrids, produces large fragrant yellow flowers.

There is also a variety of *Helleborus orientalis* (Lenten Rose) in the new garden area, primarily of the "Royal Heritage" strain. Foremost among the many color varieties is a stunning deep purple. These nodding flowers bloom in February and March, and do indeed "herald the dawn of a new season." The royal heritage strain is grown from seed in John Elsley's garden in South Carolina for Klehm's Song Sparrow Nursery. I also have some Helleborus from Sam and Carlene Jones's popular Piccadilly Farm in Watkinsville, Georgia, near Athens. They sponsor a Helleborus Day in late February that attracts lots of people to their Shade Plant Nursery. The event provides an educational experience for enthusiastic gardeners.

Returning to the pool area, to the left is a large oak-leaf hydrangea and the native *Wisteria frutescens* 'Amethyst Falls' that flowers after the Asian counterpart. To the right an upright *Ginkgo biloba* tree borders a pathway leading into what is called the "experimental garden" behind the extended *Elaeagnus* hedge. Behind the hedge is a collection of young Japanese maples seedlings along with some young 'Dooley' hydrangeas that were rooted from the parent plant by a special "cut layering" technique taught to me by my street-knowledge garden mentor, Henry.

THE EXPERIMENTAL AND PERENNIAL GARDENS

In the far corner of the experimental garden next to the fence I have put to use several of Dirr's throwaway seedlings of a golden oriental arborvitae (*Thuja orientalis*). These fast-growing specimens will soon form a thick golden fence hedge. There are other specimen plants in the experimental garden area, the most notable being an oriental fringe tree (*Chionathus retusus*) called 'Tokyo Tower' for its upright form. Skyscraper-type plants are welcomed in a garden running out of space!

Coming out of the experimental garden, the terrain slopes sharply downward to the sunroom. The steep slope presented a rapid-water-flow challenge, which was addressed with the installation of huge stone steps, another of Ron Deal's designs. This hardscape solved the wash problem and opened up the best perennial garden in the entire complex. There are a variety of dahlias, echinaceas, verbenas, sedums, and coreopsis, to name a few perennials. Armitage calls me when he has a few throwaway annuals to fill the area with color. The plant that gets the most attention is a spreading and colorful Asiatic jasmine (*Trachelospermum* asiaticum) called 'Snow in Summer', which lights up the ground in the hot summer months with its white, green, and pink foliage.

At the bottom of the perennial garden close to the sunroom is the blue Atlas cedar (*Cedrus atlantica* 'Glauca'), trained to form an arch over a pathway. Directly behind and towering over the cedar is a rapid-growing dawn redwood (*Metasequcia glyptostroboides*) given to me by Paul

The Terrace Garden with Helleborus

Cappiello while he was working with the Bernheim Arboretum in Clermont, Kentucky, south of Louisville. As noted earlier, Cappiello is a Dirr disciple trained under the guru. To the right is a water feature containing several water plants, including water lilies, lotuses, and the yellow flag iris. This area is complimented by a 'Golden Fullmoon' Japanese maple and a couple of laceleaf maples 'Seiryu' and 'Crimson Queen', upright and spreading, respectively, located directly behind and to the right of the cascading waterfall.

Next to the pond is a small bronzed statue called *Nina*, who is lying prone next to the waterfall, soaking in the ambience while enjoying a good book. Across the pond, her brother *Billy* is sitting on a rock and fishing.

THE SHADE GARDEN

Past the pond, one is led through a gate and introduced to one of the largest Japanese maples in the garden, another seedling gift from Mary Hardman's Commerce home. Directly to the left of the maple is a path crossing a footbridge. The path follows the dry rock stream into a shade garden. The entrance to the shade garden is called "weepers

Rhododendron 'Admiral Semmes' in the Terrace Garden

corner" because of the many varieties of small weeping plants in the area. Among the weepers are a weeping Katsura (*Cercidiphyllum japonicum*) called 'Morioka Weeping', a weeping Japanese maple (*Acer japonicum* 'Green Cascade'), a weeping Hackberry (*Celtis sinensis*), and even a weeping privet, *Ligustrum sinense* 'Emerald Mop'. The entrance path to the shade garden is framed by 'Acoma' crape myrtle (*Lagerstroemia indica* × *L. fauriei*) and a Callaway garden introduction crabapple (*Malus prunifolia* 'Callaway'). The rock-stream path features a variety of *Camellia japonica*, a very old and interesting crape myrtle, found while clearing the area, with beautiful exfoliating bark, as well as a variety of hostas, ferns, trilliums, and other plants ideally suited for the shaded area. The plant that gets a lot of attention is a spotted leopard plant (*Ligularia dentata*). Close by is a relative called *Farfugium giganteum*; the last name aptly describes the giant, rounded, glossy leaves. Armitage refers to it as "that green thing." But I like it and its cousin, the leopard plant. Both are shaded by a weeping Japanese maple 'Crimson Queen'. The maple cascades over a small mound that was built to replace a Ron Deal pond that always leaked. The mound is planted with black and yellow mondo grass and is topped

by a weeping snowbell (*Styrax japonicus* 'Carilon'). The entire area is shaded by two *Magnolia stellata* (Star) with over twenty fragrant white-to-pink tepals to a flower that opens in March.

Before leaving the shade garden, mention should be made of Dirr's favorite "quiz plant" that is located along the dry creek. If one can identify this plant, they go to the head of Dr. Dirr's class. The plant is *Dirca palustris*, called leatherwood because the stems are like leather and capable of tying in a knot without damaging the bark. The Indians used the bark for fishing lines and bowstrings. This interesting native plant likes a mostly shady area and is ideally suited for the shady dry-stream garden.

THE RUSTIC BRIDGE CROSSING

The path leads to a golden-raintree (*Koelreuteria paniculata*) with summer yellow flowers, yellow-brown seed capsules, and fall yellow leaves. The raintree stands guard in front of a rustic bridge that crosses the main creek into the *Camellia japonica* garden. In addition to some other camellia favorites previously mentioned, the winter garden contains other favorites. Everyone should have the hardy *Camellia reticulata* 'Frank Houser' as well as the variegated form that produces those enormous red/white peonylike flowers (from the inspiration of the Bill Fickling garden). Another hardy *C. reticulata* species 'Francie L', with large rose-pink undulating (wavy) petals, is a welcome addition. I have several of another favorite 'Royal Velvet'. This rapid-growing *C. japonica* with ruby red, semidouble velvety large flowers is a real winner.

What really starts the *Camellia japonica* garden off is 'Daikagura' that blooms in my garden in early October even before the earliest sasanquas. This antique peony-form, bright pink Camellia dares to be considered "one of the greatest camellias of all times!"

Camellia japonica 'Royal Velvet'

Ligularia dentata
Leopard Plant

Another antique *Camellia japonica* 'Mathothiana' ('Purple Dawn') that dates back to 1840 when it arrived in Charleston, South Carolina, adds much to the winter garden with its formal double-red blooms.

Nuccio's Nursery in California produces some of the best camellias. I have the perfect white formal double 'Nuccio's Gem' as well as the formal double coral pink 'Nuccio's Cameo'. Another Nuccio favorite is the large peony red-flowered 'Kramers Supreme' that is indeed supreme.

At the top of the camellia walk is a small dwarf conifer rock garden guarded at the entrance by the upright contorted blue Atlas cedar, *Cedrus atlantica* 'Glauca'. Several of the dwarf conifers came from the famous Iseli Nursery in Boring, Oregon. I have experimented with a variety of unique dwarf conifers from around the country. They do fine as long as they are not stressed with a water crisis, which will and did happen. Native dwarf conifers are tougher, so now all of my rock garden plants are trained in southern humidity.

Turning to the right, away from the rock garden, one finds a large contorted European filbert (*Corylus avellana* 'Contorta', 'Harry Lauder's Walking Stick') that is surrounded by several hollies of the 'Red Holly' series (*Ilex* 'Oak leaf',

I. 'Little Red', I. 'Festive', I. 'Cardinal', and I. 'Robin', the best of the series). The large, very dark, shiny green leaves of 'Robin' are outstanding. There is also a yellow-berried holly, *Ilex attenuata* 'Longwood Gold', a colorful addition to the holly grove. In the area is also a cluster of bottlebrush buckeye (*Aesculus parviflora*) and a wide variety of viburnums. Dr. Dirr has written a book on this "great group of plants" and affectionately said that a "garden without viburnums is akin to life without music and art." Consequently I have a wide variety of viburnums, such as the doublefile *Viburnum plicatum* f. *tomentosum*. 'Mariesii' and 'Shasta' are characterized by the flat, layered branches where the flowers and berries form an attractive resting place. *Viburnum plicatum* f. *plicatum* is the snowball-type such as 'Kern's Pink' or 'Mary Milton', but 'Popcorn' is the real favorite. The most spectacular of the snowball varieties is the Chinese snowball, *Viburnum macrocephalum*, which now is some fourteen feet tall and wide, producing hundreds of large white mophead flowers in the early spring that are often mistaken for hydrangeas, which bloom of course in late May and early June. My real favorite are those viburnums that have fragrance, such as *Viburnum carlesii* (Koreanspice) and the many fragrant offspring this parent

Viburnum plicatum f. *tomentosum* 'Shasta'
Doublefile Viburnum

has produced, such as its marriage to Burkwood viburnum to produce 'Mohawk' and 'Anne Russell'.

At the top of the hill as part of the winter treat, two small dogwood trees (*Cornus officinalis*) often called Cornel dogwood, light up the area with hundreds of small fluffy yellow flowers before the leaves break. In the same area is a paw paw tree (*Asimina triloba*) that displays petite purple flowers in the spring that turn into elongated edible paw paw fruits. Up next to the road by a Virginia pine (*Pinus virginiana*) is a twenty-five-feet-high black locust (*Robinia pseudoacacia*), not your usual best ornamental, but this one, 'Frisia', has golden leaves that last most of the summer, giving this locust a distinctive quality.

Taking the path downhill, toward the creek and on the left are two of the latest large collections of Japanese maples, courtesy of friendly Fred Hooks who showed up one day a few years ago with his son, a Georgia student at the time, unloading a shipment of mature maples from Oregon. What a treat! One is the must-have 'Katsura' maple, which opens in the spring with its brilliant yellow leaves, and the other is the variegated 'Otome Zakura', a nice compliment to the Katsura. To the right of the maples, toward the creek, is a magnolia 'Ballerina' seedling (*Magnolia* ×*loebneri*), a gift from Dr. Dirr, who secured the small tree from his associate, the late professor Joe McDaniels, while at the University of Illinois. The fragrant white-with-pale-pink-flush flowers contain over thirty sepals! In front of the two maples facing the lawn is the collection of Endless Summer® hydrangeas, compliments of Bailey Nursery after their three-day film shoot at the house. Further down is a tea viburnum (*Viburnum setigerum*), the best-fruited of all the viburnums, which cascades in multiple red berries in the fall toward the Endless Summer® hydrangea collection. Located just below is a spreading yoshino cherry (*Prunus* ×*yedoensis*) of the pure white-flowered Washington, D.C. tidal-basin cherry blossom fame. The cherry shades a cluster of *Fothergilla major* and *F. gardenii* that puts on a spectacular fall leaf show of red, orange, or scarlet.

Close to the creek is a fourteen-foot evergreen dogwood (*Cornus omeiensis* 'Mountain Moon') that is covered with numerous white bracts from top to bottom during mid-June. Also next to the creek is a winter-blooming viburnum called 'Dawn' (*Viburnum* ×*bodnantense*) that produces blush pink and white flowers with high fragrance in February before the leaves appear. The rest of the area by the creek is planted with hydrangeas ('Dooley' and 'Veitchii' seedlings and several large rhododendrons) shaded by a twenty-foot Japanese maple seedling. Both the rhodendrons and the Japanese maple are yet another of Mary Hardman's Commerce home garden gifts. Also along the creek are two large loblolly pines (*Pinus taeda*) with climbing hydrangeas (*Hydrangea anomala* subspecies *petiolaris*) creeping up the trunk. The pines are the foundation of two planting beds with a mass of single Knock Out® roses. In one island is a Korean stewartia (*Stewartia koreana*) with attractive exfoliating bark that produces white camellia-like single flowers in June. The other island features a Celestial® dogwood (*Cornus* × *rutgersensis* 'Rutdan'), a cross between the *C. florida* and *C. kousa*.

Returning to the lawn in front of the house are two white Japanese bridges I had built many years ago after visiting Japan long before getting the gardening infection. Crossing the creek via the Japanese bridge to the right, facing the house, requires strolling under (sometimes ducking) a cascading branch of a fascinating weeping Katsura tree called 'Amazing Grace'. This "amazing" Katsura tree (*Cercidphyllum japonicum*) bows toward a variety of weeping shrubs and trees on both sides of what is called "weepers creek." I have told many a tour group that I called it weepers creek because, after football games we lost, I would go out and weep by the creek. I must admit, on many occasions I felt like weeping with the weepers.

Among the weepers starting at the rustic bridge is a weeping yaupon holly (*Ilex vomitoria*)—so called since it was reported that Indians used the leaves to purge themselves while gearing up for a warpath. Across the creek next to a rhododendron is a hardy-orange (*Poncirus trifoliata*) with devastating-looking hooked spines. However, it does produce attractive small yellow fruit in the fall. There is also an upright weeping redbud (*Cercis canadensis*) called 'Covey' (Lavender Twist™). Next to the first white Japanese bridge and across from the Katsura tree is a six-foot weeping European larch (*Larix decidua*—since it is deciduous). Next to the larch is a weeping winged elm (*Ulmus alata* 'Lace Parasol'). Directly across is a weeping honeylocust (*Gleditsia triacanthos* f. *inermis* 'Emerald Cascade'). Interestingly, the species form of honeylocust (I have a yellow one called 'Sunburst') is the only remaining "witness tree" to President Lincoln's Gettysburg Address (November 19, 1863). In the fall of 2008, the Gettysburg honeylocusts almost became a "battlefield casualty" when a violent storm took most of the crown off, but the resilient tree has recovered and is doing well as of 2009.

Next to the honeylocusts is a weeping (somewhat) black tupelo (*Nyssa sylvatica* 'Autumn Cascades') with striking red fall color. Back across the creek, in the mass of single Knock Out® roses, is a low-spreading, multi-stemmed, weeping river birch (*Betula nigra* 'Summer Cascade'). Beside the birch next to Japanese bridge number two is another Katsura weeper called 'Tidal Wave' (in contrast to 'Amazing Grace') that has a undulating characteristic befitting its name.

The crown jewel of all these weepers is an eighteen-foot baldcypress (*Taxodium distichum*) called 'Cascade Falls'. Next to this architectural-looking dinosaur is the newest baldcypress weeper 'Falling Water', which promises to be even better. Time will tell. The new weeper is a Don Shadow introduction that he has labeled 'Falling Water', but which to Shadow's irritation some call 'Falling Waters', giving the water a plural designation.

The common baldcypress has been labeled a "stately tree," with interesting cypress knees. This deciduous conifer has good fall color and was labeled by my hometown of Mobile as the number-one survivor of the many hurricanes that have visited the Port City in the last two decades.

Next to the baldcypress is a weeping yoshino cherry (*Prunus ×yedoensis*) labeled 'Snow Fountains'. Next to the cherry with its head bowed to the creek is another weeping river birch (*Betula nigra*) 'Summer Cascade' that is trained on a single leader trunk. Interestingly it is perched under its upright river birch big brother Dura Heat™. Directly across the creek is the rapid-growing and spreading Chinese hackberry (*Celtis sinensis* 'Green Cascade'). In between this array of active weeping plants I have stuck in a few casual weeping camellias simply labeled 'Pendula'. The weeping journey ends at the driveway with a robust weeping European hornbeam (*Carpinus betulus*) that my good friend Rusty Allen from Eastside Ornamentals in Athens gave me several years ago in a five-gallon container. It is now seven feet tall with a seven-foot spread.

Next to the 'Amazing Grace' weeping Katsura tree is a cluster of Dirr's hydrangea 'Blushing Bride' that was left after the Bailey's Nursery photo shoot. These white-slightly-fading-to-pink (or light blue) mopheads attract abundant attention, particularly from the ladies who like the 'Blushing Bride' name. Directly behind 'Blushing Bride' is a maroon-foliaged mimosa silk tree (*Albizia julibrissin* Summer Chocolate™) that gives an appealing color contrast to the hydrangea haven. At the foot of the hydrangeas is a path that leads to a combination of compatible plants. The three plants are *Clethra alnifolia*, summersweet that gives off great fragrance when nothing else does in August; the red fall color extraordinaire *Fothergilla major*; and eight "blooming machines," Twist-n-Shout™ hydrangeas. I have recently put in two Asian snakebark maples (*Acer capillipes*) and Manchustriped maple (*Acer tegmentosum*), both gifts of Smithgall Woodland Garden. Both of these snakebark maples appreciate the southern magnolia tree whose shade protects their delicately thin, green-and-white-striped bark.

The southern magnolia (*Magnolia grandiflora*) is regarded by the founder of the Magnolia Society, Dr. John M. Fogg Jr., as "the most widely cultivated tree in the world." It flourishes in various zones, and my Chinese friend Donglin Zhang, a former student under Dr. Dirr and horticulture professor at the University of Maine, says it is now the most popular tree in China and has been planted all over that vast country.

Next to a statue of the four seasons (fall) is the raved-about oakleaf *Hydrangea quercifolia* 'Snowflake'. There is also a maroon-leaf Canadian red cherry (*Prunus virginiana* 'Schubert') that provides a nice contrast to several of the low-growing *Gardenia jasminoides* 'Shooting Star' seedlings. Directly under the twin magnolia path is a series of the gold variegated *Aucuba japonica* that Dirr collected on his sab-

Japanese Bridge over Weepers Creek

batical in the Hiller Arboretum garden in England in 1999. The collection is there for his observation, as are so many other plants in the Dooley-Dirr experimental garden.

Another Dirr plant (through his plant-introduction business) located under the magnolia grove is a new low-growing variegated illicium (*Illicium floridanum*) 'Pink Frost'. This natural woodland plant was introduced by Mickey Harp, a friend and a real gentleman, of Harp's Nursery in Fayetteville, Georgia. Mickey Harp and Dirr's plant-introduction company formed a partnership to introduce the plant.

The Fountain Circle Walk with Japanese seedling in fall color

made several trips with Dr. Dirr to the CANR and was impressed with the dedicated work done at the facility, but also with the numerous organizations from the nursery business that financially supported the research that has benefited the entire industry.

The last section under the magnolias is the fountain circle walk that is surrounded by most all of Dirr's new *Hydrangea macrophylla* introductions through McCorkle Nursery entitled Royal Majestics™, 'Queen of Pearls', a white mophead, 'Midnight Duchess', a black-stem mauve pink lacecap, and 'Princess Lace', a light pink/blue lacecap. Also in the fountain circle walk are hydrangeas Twist-n-Shout™ and 'Mini Penny' (a dwarf seedling of the famous 'Penny Mac' named for the late Penny McHenry, the founder of the American Hydrangea Society. 'Mini Penny' was the number-one "you gotta grow" plant in the *Southern Living* May/Spring edition of 2009.

Before leaving the hydrangea fountain circle heading for the front of the house, a sight to behold is a vista of seven Japanese maples with a variety of shapes and colors. Aligned in alternate rows, they start with 'Ryusen', the ultimate green weeper, followed by, 'Ruslyn in the Pink', 'Emperor I', the vigorous red upright, and 'Waterfall', the green dissectum weeper with long flowing leaves. Across the front steps is another green weeper 'Ao Shime No-Uchi' (Ao is green). This maple has long fingerlike leaves that turn gold in the fall. Next is 'Garnet', a vigorous spreading red dissectum, and the most popular upright growing Japanese maple today, 'Bloodgood'. During my garden walks I always have to pause there to take in the color sight, which is altered each time by the season and the position of the sun.

On both sides of the front steps are several American boxwoods (*Buxus sempervirens*). To the left of the steps are

I am always intrigued how the plant people work together for the betterment of the industry. A classic example is the Center for Applied Research, CANR, located next to McCorkle Nursery in Dearing, Georgia. This center was formed through the initiative of McCorkle Nursery, who approached the University of Georgia to create a unique research facility. The university liked the idea, and a nonprofit organization was formed whose mission was to keep Georgia and the Southeast in the forefront in plant breeding, evaluation, and introduction. I

Acer palmatum var. Dissectum atropurpureum 'Garnet'
Japanese Maple

Acer palmatum
The Anniversary Maple

two varieties of evergreen azaleas. First is the vigorous ten-feet-high 'Southern Indica' ('George L. Taber'—the large light pink variegated flower) and 'Dixie Beauty' (a deep red flower), both blooming in April. Right next to the 'Southern Indica' is the much-smaller 'Satsuki' hybrid (meaning "fifth month" in Japanese), blooming accordingly in May.

Providing shade for the azaleas is a large common mulberry (*Morus alba*) that is a favorite of Barbara's because of the unusual and lumpy gnarled character of the bark. Dirr and I wanted to take it down because of its commonality, plus my having to clean up the mulberries that make a mess of the walkway. We both backed off when Barbara's Lebanese blood got boiling as she emphatically stated, "Don't touch that tree? It has character!" We agreed—out of fear for our lives!

Across the lawn from the mulberry and near the creek is the largest Japanese maple in the garden. It is a green seedling I got at a good price from my friend John Barber at Bold Springs Nursery for our thirty-ninth wedding anniversary. It had a six-foot root ball and the tree was lowered into place by a huge crane. It looked like it had been there for thirty years. When Barbara walked out I proudly announced, "Happy anniversary!" For the first

and only time in our fifty-plus-year marriage I witnessed Barbara speechless! She slowly walked to the maple and started looking at the leaves for gold or diamonds—she is still looking! Who knows, she might have found one on the fiftieth anniversary. Meanwhile, I have not thought about another Japanese maple as an anniversary present. If I were considering a magnolia instead, I would probably have chosen the *Magnolia ×loebneri* 'Leonard Messel' located next to the driveway. It has been a vigorous grower, now eighteen feet tall, and I enjoy the fragrant, dozen pink strap-shaped tepals.

THE MATHIS GARDEN

Walking down the driveway past the 'Leonard Messel' magnolia and 'Dooley' hydrangea, on the left is the newest addition to my mini botanical garden—the Mathis garden. This area was made available by the late Mrs. William (Jeanne) Mathis, who leased the area to me for an ornamental garden. Her daughter, Mrs. Robert (Sylvia) Gibson, has continued to lease a portion of the property, but insists that the large rock outcropping in the front where Mr. Mathis proposed to Mrs. Mathis be respected.

The integrity of the engagement rock has top priority.

The garden was opened by cutting through the Japanese holly (*Ilex crenata*) hedge and planting at the entrance two weeping dissectum Japanese maples ('Inaba-Shidare'—*shidare* meaning "cascading") with beautiful purple red leaves that turn a brilliant crimson in the fall.

The entrance to the garden features a large arbor with a climbing and fragrant Confederate jasmine (*Trachelospermum jasminoides* 'Madison'), the only cold-hardy jasmine for our area in zone 7. The arbor built by Ron Deal is constructed of wrought iron with an oak-leaf-and-acorn motif. The lace ironwork was recycled from the nearby carport after it was remodeled. The entrance walkway features a rustic concrete design interspersed with dwarf liriope that separates the diamond-shaped concrete walkway. Upon entering the new garden, on the left is a magnificent single-red, cold-hardy camellia, 'Crimson Candles', hybridized by Dr. Clifford Parks, which took nineteen years to bring to fruition. On the right is a distinctive finger-leaf Japanese maple ('Villa Taranto') and directly in front is a dwarf red Japanese maple ('Shaina'). Directly in front of the entrance is the 'Vince Dooley' camellia—this large, single scarlet-red flower with big leaves (*C. reticulata* × *C. japonica*) was named for me by the American Camellia Society as a tribute from my good friends Dr. Buddy English and the late Dr. Dan Nathan, both highly respected camellia advocates and great University of Georgia Bulldogs!

The initial part of the Mathis garden, on a circular path, has a theme of native azaleas, deciduous oriental magnolias, hydrangeas, and of course, Japanese maples. Turning to the right of the circular path is a distinctive Japanese maple 'Shishigashira' that attracts a lot of attention with its dark green, small, crinkly leaves. A step or two further down is the fastest-growing Japanese maple I have ever seen, a Dr. Dirr introduction called 'Glowing Embers'. While making

Gazebo and *Lonicera maackii*
Amur Honeysuckle

the full circle there are several other Japanese maples: the variegated 'Butterfly', followed by two 'Omurayama' maples that are somewhat upright cascading types as opposed to the low-spreading dissectum group. I bought two because I got carried away with the new foliage of brilliant bright orange and the striking fall colors of gold and crimson. Around the circle to the right is the dark red, slow-spreading dissectum 'Tamukeyama', followed by 'Suminagashi', a red favorite with deeply divided leaves. On the left is 'Okushimo', an upright maple with odd-shaped leaves that somehow encourages deer to scrape its bark during rut. On the right, next to the fence, is 'Trompenburg', a popular maple with rich, deep, purple-red foliage.

Throughout the spring and summer, from late March to August, there is always a native azalea in bloom. In the garden circle in late March the sensuous pink-white flowered 'Piedmont' (*Rhododendron canescens*) rivals the not-so-fragrant *R. periclymenoides* 'Lavender Girl' for kicking off the season.

Several fragrant varieties follow, such as *R. atlanticum*, the multicolored Florida azalea, *R. austrinum*, and *R. arborescens*, the sweet azalea. A late spring favorite is 'Choptank Yellow', a natural hybrid from the Choptank

THE MATHIS GARDEN

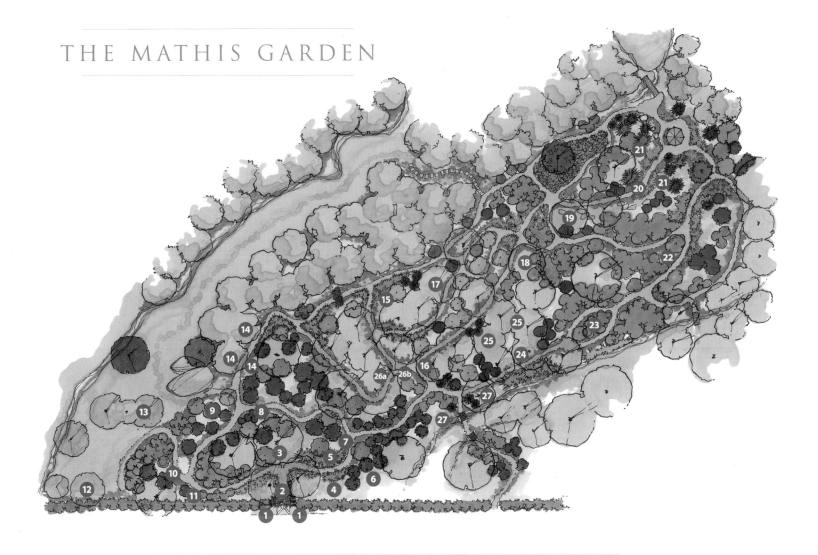

1. *Acer palmatum* var. *dissectum atropurpureum* 'Inaba Shidare'
   Japanese Maple
2. *Trachelospermum jasminoides* 'Madison'
   Confederate Jasmine
3. *Camellia* Hybrid (*C.reticulata* × *C.japonica*) 'Vince Dooley'
   Japanese Camellia
4. *Acer palmatum* 'Shishigashira'
   Japanese Maple
5. *Rhododendron* Hybrid 'My Mary'
   Native Azalea
6. *Hydrangea aspera* subspecies *sargentiana*
   Sargent Hydrangea
7. *Acer palmatum* 'Glowing Embers'
   Japanese Maple
8. *Acer palmatum* 'Omurayama'
   Japanese Maple
9. *Magnolia acuminata* 'Yellow Fever'
   Cucumbertree Magnolia
10. *Rhododendron* Hybrid 'Choptank Yellow'
    Native Azalea
11. *Magnolia acuminata* 'Elizabeth'
    Cucumbertree Magnolia

12. *Lagerstroemia fauriei* 'Fantasy'
    Fauriei Crapemyrtle
13. *Metasequoia glyptostroboides* 'Ogon'/ 'Gold Rush'
    Dawn Redwood
14. *Illicium* species collection
    Anise-tree
15. *Cornus kousa* 'Wolf Eyes'
    Kousa Dogwood
16. *Cunninghamia lanceolata* 'Glauca'
    Blue China-fir
17. *Prunus ×yedoensis*
    Yoshino Cherry
18. *Halesia diptera*
    Two-winged Silverbell
19. *Prunus incisa* × *P.campanulata* 'Okame'
    Hybrid Cherry
20. *Hydrangea paniculata* Walk
    H. paniculata Hybrid
    H. paniculata Limelight®
    Panicle Hydrangea

21. Rock Garden *Daphne odora* 'Aureomarginata'
    Winter Daphne
    Tsuga canadensis 'Pendula'
    Weeping Canadian Hemlock
22. *Hydrangea macrophylla* 'Blushing Bride'
    Bigleaf Hydrangea
23. *Calycanthus* Venus™
    Venus Sweetshrub
24. *Ginkgo biloba* 'Witches Broom'
    Maidenhair Tree
25. *Hydrangea macrophylla* remontant (reblooming) collection
    'Decatur Blue', 'David Ramey', Endless Summer®,
    'Oak Hill', 'Penny Mac', Twist-n-Shout™
26. *Cornus florida*
    A. 'Cherokee Princess'
    B. Cherokee Brave
    Flowering Dogwood
27. *Gardenia jasminoides* 'Shooting Star'
    Seedling

River in Maryland where *Rhododendron austrinum, R. atlanticum,* and *R. periclymenoides* cross-pollinate to naturally produce this fast-growing fragrant and beautiful white-flowered, yellow-splashed beauty. It is an eye- and nose-stopper.

Meanwhile the bright orange-flowered *Rhododendron calendulaceum* (Flame Azalea) catches the eyes but not the nose. There are many colorful hybrids. One of my favorites is 'My Mary', a three-species cross with large, yellow, fragrant flowers named by my good friend Jeff Beasley for his mother. Jeff and his wife, Lisa, have the best native azalea nursery in the Appalachians. Their series "Made in the Shade" is a real winner, and Jeff and Lisa have been most generous in filling my circular garden and the garden at Lake Burton with some of their very best. Two of their best have been named after their daughters—'Camilla's Blush' (Georgia graduate and medical student), a pink fragrant *R. canescens* selection, and 'Kelsey's Flame' (a Georgia "ag" student), a *R. calendulaceum* species with striking orange blossoms. To complete the ladies in the Beasley family is 'Lisa's Gold', a bright gold Florida azalea with wonderful fragrance. They have not found one yet to name after Jeff.

The grand native azalea parade reaches its grand finale with the dark red *R. prunifolium,* the hallmark of Callaway Gardens.

Sprinkled in with the magnolias, the Japanese maples, and the native azaleas are a wide variety of hydrangeas. In addition to some of the obvious old French hybrids, such as 'Mme Emile Mouillere' and 'Générale Vicomtesse de Vibraye', is the most unusual hydrangea in the garden, *H. aspera* subspecies *sargentiana.* Dr. Dirr gave the plant to me to see how it would do, and it has grown to be the tallest hydrangea in the entire garden at ten feet, with an eight-inch-wide, flat, purple fertile flower. I later found out it is practically unknown in the United States except in the far Northwest. It attracts a lot of "What is that?!" questions!

Magnolia 'Yellow Fever', in bloom

THE ASIATIC MAGNOLIA

In recent years several books have been written on the deciduous oriental magnolias and the variety is now endless. I do have a few in the circular garden that put on a gorgeous prespring show before the leaves appear.

A lap starting to the left around the circular garden reveals the following: the white-flowered *Magnolia salicifolia* (Willowleaf) with lemon-scented crushed stems, followed by 'Elizabeth', the clear yellow fragrant hybrid. Next is the purple-flowered 'Ruby', *Magnolia × soulangeana* (often referred to by many as a "tulip tree" with its goblet shaped flowers). Another saucer magnolia is 'Big Pink', with lasting and fragrant flowers. My favorite is 'Yellow Fever', which covers the twenty-feet-tall tree with big fragrant yellow flowers. Nearby is a Gresham hybrid 'Dark Shadow', with dark red purple flowers, and the summer-blooming yellow 'Hot Flash'. There is a twenty-foot *Magnolia sprengeri* 'Diva' that I have had for ten years that has yet to flower. There is also *Magnolia stellata,* the popular star magnolia 'Lyle's Legacy', with multiple white tepals. Completing the circle *Magnolia denudata* (Yulan) with white, slender-necked, gobletlike flowers that dates back to China several centuries ago.

Magnolia denudata
Yulan Magnolia

There are three trails north, east, and south that exit the circular garden and lead into other parts of the Mathis garden. The north trail in the direction of the street splits the 'Choptank Yellow' native azaleas and follows a gardenia walk. This leads into the pink hydrangea garden, all acquired from the Dirr throwaway collection upon his retirement. If any of these pinks turn another color, they will be automatically removed. In October Dirr noticed a repeat-blooming large pink mophead with coral stems that he tagged. Next to the pink hydrangea section is the pure-cinnamon-bark crape myrtle *Lagerstroemia fauriei* 'Fantasy' that is one of the parents used by the National Arboretum in Washington to produce the Indian series of crape myrtles, the most notable being 'Natchez'. 'Fantasy' crape myrtle puts on the best one-week, white, floral show in the garden, but it fades in a hurry. 'Natchez', on the other hand, will bloom for months but never display the spectacular tree-covering display of 'Fantasy'. Some other trees on the north trail garden of note are the dark-maroon-leaf flowering plum *Prunus cerasifera* 'Newport'.

In the area is the historical Kentucky coffeetree (*Gymnocladus dioicus*), a seedling from the "witness trees" where General "Stonewall" Jackson's amputated arm is buried near the Chancellorsville battlefield, where Jackson had his greatest victory. Jackson was shot and his arm amputated. He later died of pneumonia. Jackson's chaplain, Beverly Tucker Lacy, was responsible for burying the amputated arm at the Lacy family cemetery located close to the mansion of Ellwood Plantation, owned by Lacy's brother. I visited the area to view the grave site marked by a simple headstone. There are two large, handsome, Kentucky coffeetrees with their distinctive bipinnately compound leaves and ten-inch-long, leathery seed pods behind the house. I was pleased to find out the tree was so named because the early settlers of Kentucky used the seeds as a coffee substitute.

Across from the Kentucky coffeetree and next to the pink hydrangea garden is a golden dawn redwood (*Metasequoia glyptostroboides* 'Ogon'), a tree with a fascinating history. The dawn redwood originated in the age of the dinosaurs, estimated at a hundred million years ago. They became extinct except for the trees found growing on the edge of rice patties in China, from which seeds were collected in 1947 by the Arnold Arboretum. At one time it was a native to North America, so after some fifteen million years it returned to the continent after the amazing discovery and the conclusion of World War II.

Before heading east from the circular garden, reference should be made of the large collection of spreading Japanese plum yew (*Cephalotaxus harringtonia*) throughout the immediate garden area. This array was collected by a Chinese graduate student Donglin Zhang as part of his doctoral dissertation and given to me by Dirr as part of the "experimental garden." The plum yew has become quite popular among gardeners because of its heat tolerance, shade adaptability, and deer resistance.

Heading though the west path will lead the garden tourist through a collection of evergreen *Illicium* species

Illicium floridanum 'Halley's Comet'
Florida Anise Tree

(anise trees), whose leaves produce an aromatic fragrance when crushed, that gets a variety of reactions from visitors. The path goes by a ten-foot variegated Leyland cypress called 'Silver Dust' (I saw one in England that was 130 feet tall!). Behind the cypress (× *Cypressocyparis leylandii*) is a white oak (*Quercus alba*), one of my most favorite trees, with its distinctive scaly, shedding bark. I have one on the farm that's a beauty, measuring over fifty inches in circumference. There are two white oaks that are "witness trees" to the battle of Antietam near the cornfield where some of the bloodiest fighting took place during the morning of the bloodiest one-day battle of the war.

Gently the path rises to the top of the garden, where on the crest sits a gazebo. Along the way, the biggest, largest-leaved of all the deciduous magnolias, *Magnolia macrophylla*, and a *Cornus kousa* 'Wolf Eyes' (the leaves look exactly like a wolf's eye) jump out at you. Before reaching the crest, and pausing to enjoy the garden or lake scene from the gazebo, the 'Okame' cherry (*Prunus* hybrid), the first to bloom fully by the end of February with pink petals, is worth a stare. The tree was given to me by my friend and University of Georgia graduate Harold E. Bailey of the Hartwell Family Nursery.

While rocking in the gazebo, look down at the two rock gardens on each side of the path, or in the wintertime delight in the fragrance of flowers of the winter *Daphne odora*, called "the aristocrat of fragrant shrubs." In July and August, after the *Hydrangea macrophylla* fade, you can enjoy the white-flowering *Hydrangea paniculata* allèe. It is a great time to enjoy the view from the gazebo of the garden in early spring when the native dogwoods (*Cornus florida*) are in bloom.

In addition to the native flowering dogwoods (*Cornus florida*) that have been in the area for decades, I have planted a variety of some of the best flowering dogwood cultivars acquired from Dr. Dirr. All of these will perform well under the tall-pine, sun-filtered canopy. Among the best are 'Cloud 9' with pure white bracts, 'Plena' (double-white flowering), 'Cherokee Princess' (large white), and 'Cherokee Brave' (pink-to-red-bracted cultivar). Heading down to the far side from the gazebo and the ridge, most every women's garden club I have given a tour pauses and exclaims, "Wow, what is that?" Of all things, "that" is a honeysuckle (*Lonicera maackii*) that Dr. Dirr ranks in his "top five worst plants" category and classifies as a "noxious weed." There is no question that amur honeysuckle is an invasive pest, but I remember hearing from some horticulture expert that "there is a place for every plant" or "one man's weed is another man's (woman's) jewel." This "jewel" that attracts so much female attention and gives Dirr so much heartburn is loved because it forms a nice canopy and the brown, exfoliating, multi-leader stems, trunk bark, and exposed root characteristic are attractive. Besides, Barbara believes it produces a wonderful honeysuckle fragrance when in flower, in contrast to Dirr, who says there is no fragrance in amur honeysuckles. I side with my spouse over my teacher!

Coming down the path on the right along the ridge is the largest concentration of bigleaf hydrangeas in the entire garden. Most of the hydrangeas on the ridge are the reblooming (remontant) variety, such as the white mop-head 'Blushing Bride' and the blue mopheads 'David Ramsey', Endless Summer®, 'Decatur Blue', 'Oak Hill', and 'Penny Mac'; the pink lacecap Twist-n-Shout™ is also among the remontant types.

Down the ridge and along the drainage ditch are a variety of new redbud introductions highlighted by 'Hearts of Gold', a fast-growing tree appropriately named since the new growth of the heart-shaped leaves opens with a brilliant yellow color. The leaves slowly change to a light green with the summer heat. There is also a white-flowered form ('Alba') and one called 'Ace of Hearts', with the smaller leaves appearing to "stack" on top of each other. There are also the dwarf forms 'Don Egolf' (*C. chinensis*) and 'Little Woody'. Other redbuds grace the Mathis garden, such as the handsome purple leaf 'Forest Pansy' on the ridge across from the "hide and seek" children's bench sculpture. The other redbud of note is 'Appalachian Red', the reddest and longest-lasting of all the redbuds. The plant is located on the path coming down from the infamous amur honeysuckle. Other red-buds in the Dooley garden include the redbud weeper 'Traveller' that is handsome in a container by the pool. Along weepers creek is the fast-growing redbud weeper 'Covey'. Also by the pool stands one of the latest additions, 'The Rising Sun', which holds its gold color better than the rest.

I recently acquired two new variegated forms of red-bud, 'Floating Clouds' and 'Silver Cloud'. I installed them in a new area I opened up by the driveway entrance to the garden next to the Kwanzan cherry. Both are white-blotched with green leaves, but 'Floating Clouds' has var-iegations that are much more pronounced. There are many more varieties out there, and I continue to look for them, especially some of the new introductions.

The Mathis garden walk ends along the ditch walk with two interesting dwarf trees, a *Ginkgo biloba* 'Witches Broom' that has not grown over four feet tall in six years, and a sweet gum (*Liquidambar styraciflua*) about the same size, called 'Gumball'. The path leads back to the circular garden and back under the trellis to the driveway.

The entire garden is still young, and like all gardens is growing and constantly changing. I have enthusiastically adapted to that fact. I have also adapted, though somewhat less enthusiastically, to the fact that our house is growing and constantly changing, as evidenced by ten major additions. It has taken me a little longer to reconcile to the lat-est Barbara domestic brainstorm—gutting the entire part of the original house, forcing us to vacate and relocate to the pool house, where I am at this writing. I have become the garden watchdog, making sure that not a single plant is harmed by the construction. Experience has taught me that some construction workers can be rather reckless at times.

While one eye is focused on protecting the garden, the other eye is quietly searching for my next horticultural jour-ney. Enticing is the state of Oregon, where the ideal growing climate produces some of the best conifers and Japanese maple treasures in the United States. Besides, there are a lot more magnificent gardens in the world left to see.

The journey continues . . .

AFTERWORD

ALLAN M. ARMITAGE, Ph.D.

*I*f you have reached this page, you have already been moved, exhilarated, and amazed by the botanical antics of the Coach. If you skipped through the book and stopped here for the heck of it, please go back. It is a great read.

I still remember Coach walking into my classroom, carrying his notebook, and quietly sitting down in the back. I couldn't help but smile as the other students' eyes bugged out as they wondered what was going on, but no muss, no fuss; Coach was there to learn and was soon just another classmate. That was part of his strength, fitting in and quietly grasping all the knowledge he could.

I loved meeting the incredibly interesting people whom Coach found through gardening and introduces to us in these pages. I enjoyed his journeys around the state of Georgia and around the world. I felt privileged to share his new love of Japanese maples, hydrangeas, and even a few of those wimpy herbaceous plants. Vince Dooley's accomplishments as an extraordinary coach and an exceptional athletic director will always be part of his legacy. Now we can add garden ambassador, botanical scholar, and landscape guru to his *curriculum vitae*. I certainly hope you enjoyed the journey as much as I.

Georgia Living

AN INSIDER'S GUIDE TO EXPLORING YOUR STATE

Steve Penley Exhibit

MACON, GEORGIA

Little Richard's portrait hangs alongside those of Ray Charles, the Allman Brothers, James Brown, and others at the Georgia Music Hall of Fame through July 9. The Georgia-bred artist's works are bold, bright, and big. (His R.E.M. painting measures nearly 30 feet across.) *georgiamusic.org* or *478/751-3334*